CULTURE CLASH - IMMIGRANTS AND REFORMERS

1880-1920

by
Paul McBride

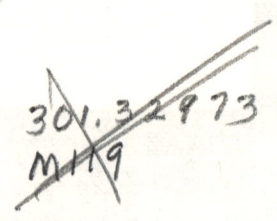

Published in 1975 by

R AND E RESEARCH ASSOCIATES
4843 Mission Street, San Francisco 94112
18581 McFarland Avenue, Saratoga, California 95070

Publishers and Distributors of Ethnic Studies
Editor: Adam S. Eterovich
Publisher: Robert D. Reed

Library of Congress Card Catalog Number

75-5331

ISBN

0-88247-361-1

Copyright 1975
by
Paul W. McBride

Dedicated to: Joey, Paula, Paul and Marc
(and all others in the process
of migration)

TABLE OF CONTENTS

	Page
PREFACE	vii

Chapter

		Page
I.	PROGRESSIVES, IMMIGRANTS AND RACISM	1
II.	SETTLEMENTS, CHARITIES, AND THE CULTURAL COLD WAR	13
III.	EDUCATORS, IMMIGRANTS, AND THE RISE OF INDUSTRIAL EDUCATION	37
IV.	THE YMCA AND THE POLITICS OF CO-OPTATION	62
V.	PETER ROBERTS: THE TRAVAILS OF A MODERATE	84

	Page
EPILOGUE	103
APPENDIXES:	
Appendix A-1	106
Appendix A-2	108
Appendix A-3	109
Appendix A-4	110
Appendix A-5	112
Appendix B-1	113
Appendix B-2	117
Appendix B-3	122
Appendix B-4	126
Appendix B-5	134
BIBLIOGRAPHY	139

PREFACE

This work combines five studies revolving around the common theme of conflict between American reformers and immigrants during the progressive era. It explores the attitudes and approaches of several urban groups and organizations working among the ethnic minorities. Someone has said that we hope according to our dreams but act according to our fears. Such was the case with those who labored to construct out of the urban malaise of the early twentieth century a more cohesive and more just society. That goal and hope was twisted and often overshadowed by the fear that immigrants threatened to undermine--even destroy--middle class values and structures. Somewhat like the nativist societies which historians have treated so unkindly (with justification), fearful reformers pressured the ethnics to purge themselves of the old world culture and conform to the new. Only in this way could they assure Americanization and avoid cultural mongrelization.

This study examines the charities, settlements, educators (particularly the industrial education movement), and the Young Men's Christian Association, each of which developed extensive programs for immigrants. According to its hopes and fears, each contributed to something approaching a cultural cold war with the strangers in their land.

To Professors Willard B. Gatewood, Alumni Professor of History at the University of Arkansas and to Charles Crowe, University of Georgia, I owe a special thanks. Their perceptive suggestions stimulated my thinking more than either of them realize. I am also indebted for friendly help and insight to Professors Robert Griffith, University of Massachusetts; Warren Kimball, Rutgers at Newark; and John Chalmers Vinson, Will Holmes and Melvin Herndon at the University of Georgia. My friend and former colleague, Professor Hugh Hammett of Rochester Institute of Technology has helped me to soften some punches and to see more clearly both sides of the issues I raise in this work.

Mrs. Virginia Downes (now in pleasant and proud retirement) and the staff of the YMCA historical library in New York City were most helpful and hospitable during my research stay there. Mrs. Dorothy Owens, manuscript typist at Ithaca College, is simply second to none. Her editing, typing, and consultation is responsible for the excellence of the final copy. My fellow-scholar in ethnic research, Adam S. Eterovich, through R & E Research Associates, as well as his own work, has contributed significantly to the discipline. For his interest in my work and his enrichment of minority studies, I am indebted to him.

Above all others, I thank my lovely wife Joanne. For her encouragement, forbearance, love, forgiveness, and a little "sweet thunder" now and then, I owe her more than I can say.

CHAPTER I

PROGRESSIVES, IMMIGRANTS AND RACISM

In one of the crueler ironies of United States history, the earlier years of the twentieth century brought into discordant juxtaposition the high tides of racism and immigration. During the first decade, nearly nine million foreigners journeyed to the United States. Almost three quarters of these traced their heritage to eastern and southern Europe.[1] Unhappily for these "new" immigrants, neither before nor since have Americans of the dominant middle class been more suspicious or hostile towards peoples of strange colors, creeds, and nationalities.

Setting the tone for America's reaction to the newcomers was a decidedly unreceptive intellectual atmosphere. Social Darwinism, eugenics, theories of Anglo-Saxon supremacy, and dire warnings of race suicide convinced most educated Americans, progressive and conservative alike, that their nation and its institutions were in danger. All of these intellectual currents contributed to the ground swell of racism which so detrimentally affected the relations between native Americans and the foreign born.[2]

---

[1] Henry Steele Commager, Samuel Eliot Morison and William E. Leuchtenberg, *The Growth of the American Republic* (New York: Oxford University Press, 1969), Vol. II, p. 108.

[2] The best single account of the impact of social Darwinism is still Richard Hofstadter, *Social Darwinism in American Thought* (New York: Braziller, 1959); Also important on this topic are Henry Steele Commager, *The American Mind* (New Haven: Yale University Press, 1950), Thomas F. Gossett, *Race: the History of an Idea in America* (Dallas, Texas: Southern Methodist University, 1963), and Eric F. Goldman, *Rendevous With Destiny* (New York: Alfred A. Knopf, 1952). On the European origins of racism and Anglo-Saxonism see Hannah Arendt, *The Origins of Totalitarianism* (New York: Harcourt Brace and World, 1966), pp. 158-59. Robert Wiebe, *The Search for Order* (New York: Hill and Wang, 1967), places racism and social Darwinism in the context of a deeply disturbed, changing, and insecure American society. These subjects will be examined in detail in the course of this and subsequent chapters. On "race suicide," see especially the writings of Francis A. Walker particularly "The Growth of the United States," *Century*, XXIV (August, 1882), pp. 920-26; "Immigration," *Yale Review*, I (August, 1892),

In their concern for the alleged Anglo-Saxon and Teutonic origins of American institutions, historians during the Progressive years contributed significantly to intellectual racism. The outspoken Teutonists John Fiske, John W. Burgess, and Henry Cabot Lodge, though historians only in the loosest sense, considerably influences historical scholarship during the Progressive era. Fiske became the first president of the Immigration Restriction League and served from 1894 to 1897. Lodge, also a league member, six times guided through Congress the literacy test, designed to limit immigration. Burgess, a noted political scientist, also championed the cause of immigration restriction. As writers of history, all three assumed that the "greatness" of the United States, her "resilience," "industriousness," "love of liberty" and "spirit of good will" (and other equally ill-defined terminology) could be traced directly to the forests of Germany or the shores of England. These amorphous doctrines held that only peoples of Anglo-Saxon or Teutonic heritages really belonged in America.[3]

John Fiske, in *Virginia and Her Neighbors,* explained Teutonism as well as any historian could without the benefit of any research on the subject. Only "ruffians and boors" comprised those who were not of

---

pp. 125-45; "Immigration and Degradation," *Forum,* XI (August, 1891), pp. 634-44; and "The United States Census," *Forum,* XI (May, 1891), pp. 258-67. The best general accounts of immigration restriction are Barbara Solomon, *Ancestors and Immigrants* (Cambridge, Mass.: Harvard University Press, 1956) and John Higham, *Strangers In the Land* (New Brunswick, N.J.: Rutgers University Press, 1955).

[3]For Fiske's ideas of Teuton supremacy consult his *The Critical Period in American History* (Boston and New York: Houghton Mifflin Company, 1916); *Old Virginia and Her Neighbors* (2 vols.; Boston and New York: Houghton Mifflin Company, 1902); and *The Beginnings of New England: or, The Puritan Theocracy in Its Relations to Civil and Religious Liberty* (Boston and New York: Houghton Mifflin Company, 1899). Lodge exhalted his Norman ancestry in the context of Teutonism particularly in his *Early Memories* (New York: Macmillan, 1913); and *A Short History of the English Colonies in America* (New York: Macmillan, 1881). His writings and speeches on the topic of immigration seem endless. See, for example, Lodge's "The Restriction of Immigration," *North American Review,* CLII (January, 1891), pp. 27-36; "Census and Immigration," *Century Magazine,* XLVI (September, 1893), pp. 737-39; and "Lynch Law and Unrestricted Immigration," *North American Review,* CLII (May, 1891), pp. 602-12. John W. Burgess effectively spread the gospel of Teutonic superiority in his famous classes in the history of political institutions at Columbia University. By far the best synthesis of the historians of this period concerning the subject of immigration is Edward N. Saveth, *American Historians and European Immigrants 1875-1925* (New York: Russell and Russell, 1948). See also Solomon, *Ancestors and Immigrants,* Chapters I and II.

the right "pedigree."[4] Curiously, none of these writers felt it necessary to clarify exactly what they meant by Aryan, Nordic, Teuton or Anglo-Saxon stock. They used the terms interchangeably and with bewilderingly little explanation. Probably the most revealing definition was given by John W. Burgess who said, "Anybody can tell an Anglo-Saxon. . . . An Anglo-Saxon is a man who instinctively knows that liberty cannot survive trade unions and other socialistic schemes from Eastern Europe."[5]

The elitist hue inherent in Teutonism obviously colored the historians' attitude toward the new immigrants about whom they engaged in the most tenuous generalizations. John Burgess, lamenting the arrival of the Eastern Europeans to American shores, asserted, "They are inclined to anarchy and crime. . . . They are, in everything which goes to make up folk character, the exact opposite of Americans."[6]

Nor did the advent of the environmentalist historians led by Frederick Jackson Turner reverse the anti-immigrant outlook of the historian. Turner's challenge to the theory of Teutonic origins and his emphasis on the environment as a molder of American character and institutions actually worked in just the opposite way. Not only were the new immigrant groups not of the right pedigree, but they settled in the city where they could not benefit from the rigor of the frontier process.[7] Turner himself, despite unbounded faith in the frontier melting pot, doubted the assimilability of the newer groups because they usually settled in the cities. He noted in 1907 that "The free lands that made the process of assimilation easy have gone. The immigration is becoming increasingly more difficult of assimilation . . . [its] effects upon American social well-being are dangerous in the extreme."[8] He referred

---

[4] Fiske, *Virginia*, Vol. II, p. 26.

[5] Quoted in Eric F. Goldman, *Rendevous with Destiny* (New York: Alfred A. Knopf, 1965), p. 89.

[6] Quoted in Saveth, *American Historians and Immigration*, p. 49.

[7] The essays in Turner's, *The Frontier in American History* (New York: Holt, Rinehart and Winston, 1962) provide a convenient source of his ideas on immigration. Also enlightening is a series of articles Turner wrote for the *Chicago Record Herald* between August 28 and October 16, 1901, discussed in Saveth, *American Historians and Immigration*, pp. 127-32.

[8] Quoted in Saveth, *American Historians and Immigration*, p. 132.

to the new immigrant as "tides of alien immigrants . . . replacing the old stock . . . [lowering] the standard of living . . . invading democracy . . . the dull brains of great masses of these unfortunates from southern and eastern Europe. . . ."[9] Thus, the frontier hypothesis with its emphasis on environmentalism rather than racial origins helped to degrade rather than exalt the new immigrant. The noted progressive activist and academician, John R. Commons, assured his readers:

> It is not conceivable that the immigrants of the present day from Southern Europe and Asia could have succeeded as frontiersmen and pioneers in the settlement of this country.[10]

Edward A. Ross, another paragon of progressivism, with a doff of the hat to Turner, accused the new immigrant of effecting the "submergence of the pioneering breed."[11]

While historians contributed to and were part of the racism of their era, they devoted little effort to the study of immigration. Immigration history had yet to be born. Professor Edward N. Saveth has correctly pointed out that between 1875 and 1925, historians:

> Had hardly more than an occasional insight into the role of immigration in our national development. When they treated the subject of European immigration at all, they treated it as a sort of historiographic hangnail--a side issue to which little attention need be paid.[12]

The reasons for the historian's indifference to immigration are relatively clear. Many historians avoided the topic because current controversial issues did not lend themselves to "impartial scholarship." As one historian warned, "Above all else, he (the allegedly impartial scholar) must avoid an appearance of lending himself to the support

---

[9]"Pioneer Ideals and the State University," in Turner, *Frontier*, pp. 277-78.

[10]John R. Commons, *Race and Immigration in America* (New York: Macmillan, 1920), pp. 127-28.

[11]Edward A. Ross, *The Old World in the New* (New York: Century, 1914), p. 282. See also his *Changing America* (New York: Century, 1912).

[12]Saveth, *American Historians and Immigration*, p. 9.

of popular clamor."[13] Furthermore, activist Progressive historians such as Charles A. Beard were absorbed in studying the economic undercurrents of the American past rather than ethnic-cultural issues. Perhaps more important still, most historians were white, Anglo-Saxon, Protestant and upper or middle class. Historians more akin to the new immigrants and therefore more interested and sympathetic with them had not yet arrived on the professional scene. In short, the historians of the progressive era ignored the immigrant because they reflected the prejudices of their class and nationality.

As academicians promoting racism, the historians had plenty of company during the progressive years. Other disciplines, such as criminal anthropology, phrenology, and eugenics developed strong racial overtones which received added support from social Darwinism. The sciences were perhaps most influential because the progressive era was so dominated by science and technology. Robert Wiebe has made a strong case for the progressive era being characterized by a search for order.[14] Progressives indeed created a cult of order and efficiency whose patron saints were science and technology. Unfortunately for the teeming immigrants, this merger of the progressive and the scientific mentality produced a racism which attracted university professors, progressive dandies, social, charity and settlement workers, YMCA organizers, Brahmin elites, and southern rednecks. All of these were searching for their own kind of order.

An interesting case in point is the eugenics movement which spread through the scientific community after 1900. Eugenics drew heavily on the fields of criminal anthropology and phrenology, which were partially concerned with tracing hereditary criminal traits. According to this approach, troublesome characteristics such as idleness, orneriness or hot temperment were inherited. Thus, the noted phrenologist Caesar Lombroso assured American intellectual circles that the criminal was "an atavistic beast whose behavior could no more be changed than his atypical brain . . . the pauper's dependency is as incorrigible as his deformed jaw and teeth."[15]

---

[13] O. G. Libby in *Mississippi Valley Historical Review*, I (January, 1914), p. 16.

[14] Robert H. Wiebe, *The Search for Order 1877-1920* (New York: Hill and Wang, 1967).

[15] Mark Haller, *Eugenics* (New Brunswick, N.J.: Rutgers University Press, 1963), p. 41. An account of the impact of criminal anthropology and phrenology on American thought is provided in Arthur E. Fink, *Causes of Crime: Biological Theories in the United States 1800-1915* (Philadelphia: University of Pennsylvania Press, 1938). An overview of scientific racism is cogently provided in Thomas F. Gossett, *Race: The History of an Idea in America* (Dallas, Texas: Southern Methodist University Press, 1963). On the European origins of racism see

The early course of the eugenics movement in the United States was largely determined by Charles B. Davenport. Davenport and others founded the American Breeders Association in 1903 which fostered Mendelian research in animal breeding. In 1906, he established within that organization the Committee on Eugenics to "emphasize the value of superior blood and the menace to society of inferior blood."[16] In 1904 the Carnegie Institute sponsored the Station for Experimental Evolution at Cold Spring Harbor, Long Island, and appointed Davenport as director. He immediately established a special committee on deaf-mutism, feeble-mindedness, insanity, inheritance of mental traits, criminality, epilepsy, and immigration. To head the Committee on Immigration Davenport appointed Prescott Hall and Robert Ward--two founders of the Immigration Restriction League a decade before. Armed with a large endowment from a wealthy Brahmin, Mrs. E. H. Harriman, Davenport also founded the Eugenics Records Office near Cold Spring Harbor in 1910. By 1924 the office had trained 258 case workers to gather data on family trees and to trace the inheritance of both mental and physical characteristics. But Davenport's approach was distinctly American. While the world eugenic movement began to recognize the extreme complexity and interrelationships of human characteristics, Davenport and his trainees searched for simple Mendelian proportions for such human traits as "inadventuresomeness, unconversationableness, matter of factness, occupational interests and reading habits."[17]

The activities of the eugenics movement dovetailed nicely with the patriotic societies which mushroomed during the reform era. David Starr Jordan, then president of Indiana University, and chairman of Davenport's eugenics committee, frequently spoke to patriotic societies and praised them in his book *The Human Harvest*. He asserted that the assumptions of the patriotic societies were praiseworthy because "the revolutionary fathers were a superior breed of man . . . to have had such names in our personal ancestry is of itself a case for thinking more highly of ourselves."[18] The many eugenics organizations which began early in the century in almost every major city, such as the Race Betterment Society in Battle Creek and the Galton Society in New York, became centers of elite racist thinking. Two members of the Galton Society were Lothrop Stoddard and Madison Grant who achieved distinction

---

Hannah Arendt, *The Origins of Totalitarianism* (New York: Harcourt, Brace and World, 1966), pp. 158-89. See also Richard Hofstadter, *Social Darwinism in American Thought* (New York: Braziller, 1959), *passim*, and John Higham, *Strangers in the Land* (New Brunswick, N.J.: Rutgers University Press, 1955), Chapter VI for standard accounts of the intellectual history of racism.

[16]Quoted in Haller, *Eugenics*, p. 62.

[17]Quoted from Charles P. Davenport, *The Trait Book*, Eugenics Records Office, Bulletin No. 6 (New York: Cold Springs Harbor, 1912) in Haller, *Eugenics*, p. 67.

[18]David Starr Jordan, *The Human Harvest: A Study of the Decay*

as prolific racist propagandists.

Eugenics caught the enthusiasm of the reform generation partly because it promised quick results. Where social Darwinism envisaged gradual passive evolutionary reform, eugenics asserted that utopia was just around the corner, a utopia in which the elite could feel comfortable. Charles Van Hise, president of the University of Wisconsin, bragged in 1914, "We know enough about eugenics so that if the knowledge were applied the defective classes would disappear within a generation."[19] Thus, eugenics offered a short cut to order and security by quickly eliminating the degenerates of society.

The relation between eugenics and racism is obvious. More important to an understanding of the reform era is the relation between racism and progressivism. Not only were such reformers as Richard T. Ely, John R. Commons and Edward A. Ross anti-immigrant on racist grounds, but so too were Presidents, Theodore Roosevelt and Woodrow Wilson. Though representing conflicting streams of progressivism, Roosevelt and Wilson evidently agreed with the scientific racism of their time.

Theodore Roosevelt's historical writings were strongly influenced by Teutonist and elitist theories.[20] But a more important indication of his attitudes on race were his actions as president. Roosevelt was privately very sympathetic to the Immigration Restriction League. One of the "confidential advisors to the president on immigration matters"[21] was James B. Reynolds, a vice-president of the league. In 1906, Roosevelt appointed James Patton, probably the most outspoken league restrictionist, to investigate Ellis Island. Patton was the league's liaison and chief spokesman to the more vitriolic, anti-Catholic, and patriotic societies such as the Junior Order of Mechanics.[22] Furthermore, Roosevelt's actions in appointing the Immigration Commission in 1906 strongly suggested that he agreed with the restriction league. According to his instructions to Speaker, Joseph B. Cannon, Roosevelt expected that the commission would "put before Congress a plan which would amount to a definite solution to this immigrant

---

of Races Through the Survival of the Unfit (Boston: American Unitarian Association, 1907), p. 104. See also his *Imperial Democracy* (New York: D. Appleton Company, 1899).

[19] Quoted in Haller, *Eugenics*, p. 67.

[20] Saveth, *American Historians and Immigration*, pp. 112-22.

[21] Solomon, *Ancestors and Immigrants*, p. 196.

[22] *Ibid.*, pp. 124-26. Solomon contends that the Immigration Restriction League closely cooperated with the fringe patriotic organizations but that it publicized the relationship as little as possible.

business."[23] The president appointed as experts on immigration, Jeremiah W. Jenks, a prominent restrictionist, Charles P. Neill, his own commissioner of labor, and William R. Wheeler, a Republican politician from San Francisco where the Japanese problem was at its peak. At a cost of three years time, the labor of three hundred staff workers, the compiling of forty-two volumes and the investment of one million dollars, the commission vented its own preconceptions.[24]

Perhaps Roosevelt's racism and elitism were most apparent in his private correspondence. To the eugenicist Charles B. Davenport, with whom he was in great sympathy, the president wrote:

> Someday we will realize that the prime duty, the
> inescapable duty, of the good citizen of the right
> type is to leave his or her blood behind him in
> the world; and that we have no business to permit
> the perpetuation of citizens of the wrong type.[25]

Furthermore, Roosevelt's detente politics with the leaders of the business world, of which Professor Gabriel Kolko has written,[26] makes a little more sense when one realizes that the president considered them "citizens of the right type." In retrospect, Roosevelt's New Nationalism was closer akin to the racism of Madison Grant than to the humanism of Lillian Wald.

Nor did President Woodrow Wilson substantially disagree with Roosevelt on racial matters. In his *History of the American People*, Wilson roundly condemned the races of the new immigrant stock as, "men of the lowest class from the south of Italy and men of the meaner sort out of Hungary and Poland." He felt that even the Chinese were better than "most of the coarse crew that came crowding in every year at the

---

[23] Oscar Handlin, "Old Immigrant and New," in *Race and Nationality in American Life* (Boston: Little, Brown & Co., 1948), p. 95. In this essay Handlin offers devastating criticism of the commissions findings and methodology. He further questions Roosevelt's motives in appointing such biased commission members.

[24] For an account in general agreement with Handlin, see Solomon, *Ancestors and Immigrants*, Chapter VII.

[25] Roosevelt to Davenport, quoted in Haller, *Eugenics*, p. 81.

[26] Gabriel Kolko, *The Triumph of Conservatism* (New York: The Free Press of Glencoe, 1963).

eastern ports."[27] Statements such as these caused him no end of embarrassment when he was running for office. Furthermore, the evidence suggests that Wilson vetoed the literacy test in 1915 not because of the profound principles which he publicized but for political reasons. To Senator John Sharp Williams of Mississippi, Wilson apologetically explained that he had to veto the literacy test bill because of the "most explicit statements" he had made "to groups of our fellow citizens of foreign extraction," and despite his finding it "distasteful" to have to do it.[28]

Elitism, scientific racism, and the chilling fear that American institutions were endangered defined the progressive response to the new immigrants. The Immigration Restriction League roster reads like a Who's Who of progressivism.[29] The presidents of the progressive era generally supported its pronouncements.

This study will examine several reform groups in their reaction to and relations with the immigrants. Specifically, it will study the charity and settlement movements, the educators, particularly the advocates of industrial education, and finally an urban religious organization, the Young Men's Christian Association. All of these groups related to the new immigrants within the framework of the fear, racism, and elitism of the reform era. All demanded of the immigrant an almost immediate adherence to white, middle-class, Anglo-Saxon traditions. Consequently, they engaged in a cultural cold war with the strangers in the land--a war in which victory was defined as the surrendering of old world traditions, institutions and heroes.

No matter how earnestly the charity worker, settlement volunteer, educator, or YMCA operative tried to help the foreigner, he could not escape his fear and cultural contempt. The founder of Boston's South End House complained of the immigrants' "unspeakable, degraded standard

---

[27] Woodrow Wilson, *A History of the American People* (New York: Harper Brothers, 1902), Vol. IV, pp. 212-14. An excellent evaluation of Wilson's historical writings is given by Saveth, *American Historians and Immigration*, pp. 137-49. See also Higham, *Strangers in the Land*, pp. 139, 191-93, and 203.

[28] Arthur S. Link, *Woodrow Wilson and the Progressive Era* (New York, Harper Row, 1954), p. 61.

[29] Among the more prominent were Franklin H. Giddings, Franklin MacVeagh (National Civic Federation), James B. Reynolds (Lawyer, Sociologist), Robert A. Woods (Boston's prominent social worker and founder of South End House), E. A. Ross, John R. Commons, and the presidents of Harvard, Stanford, Georgia Tech, University of Chicago, Randolph Macon, Western Reserve, Bowdoin College. Many of these men represented the progressive pulse of the nation. See Solomon, *Ancestors and Immigrants*, Chapter VII.

of life," which represented a "contaminating mixture" to those of the "vigorous Anglo-Saxon Race."[30] Joseph Lee, a leader of tenement reform in Boston revealed that:

> The idea is not that we, the rich, out of our great goodness and kindness of heart should help you, the poor, but that we . . . insist on being proud of the sort of citizen we produce, for the honor of the family we cannot have rags and drunkenness.[31]

The Boston Associated Charities basically concurred with Lee's elitism. It led a move among charity and social work groups in other cities to endorse and promote the work of the Immigration Restriction League. One discouraged charity volunteer complained that "immigration laws have allowed many to come to America for whom there is no place and charity has kept them alive here."[32] Furthermore, a study of *Charities*, the weekly journal of the charity organizations of the United States, reveals something less than a charitable and sympathetic approach to the poor and foreign.[33]

All of the groups examined in this study were involved, in one way or another, in educating the foreigner. Public schools, settlement houses, and the YMCA each developed Americanization programs designed to reculturize the immigrant. Their ideas cross fertilized one another. Thus, each group promoted industrial education not only to meet the demands of industrial technology, but to inculcate those kinds of attitudes

---

[30] Quoted in Solomon, *Ancestors and Immigrants*, p. 141.

[31] *Ibid.*, p. 139.

[32] *Ibid.*, p. 137.

[33] For examples of hostility or lack of sympathy for the poor and the foreign, see Rev. George Hodge, "On Pauperism," *Charities*, II (December 3, 1898), p. 7; Robert T. Paine, "The Importance of Stopping Outdoor Relief to Chronic or Hereditary Paupers," *Charities* X (February 7, 1903), pp. 134-37; and Bertha Baruch's report to the Patriots League in *Charities* XXVIII (September 14, 1912), p. 748. The number of articles hostile to immigrants seem to increase after the Immigration Commission made public its findings in 1911. For a revealing insight into the mind of the charity worker, read the discussion centering on what to do about the unclean of mind, the "foul of mouth and deprived of heart" in New York state's almshouses. New York State, *Second Annual Conference of Charities and Corrections, 1902* (Albany: J. B. Lyon and Company, 1902), pp. 38-50.

which would promote complacency, docility and industrial efficiency in the foreigner.

The reform groups analyzed here joined most Americans in refusing to approach the immigrant in other than their own terms. Labor saw the immigrant as a threat to its well-being. Business leaders, at least after the Haymarket affair, began to see the immigrant as a carrier of disorder and radicalism. The prohibitionist saw him as a drunkard.[34] In general, Americans yearning for security and order demanded that something be done about the immigrant. Robert DeCoursey Ward, the noted restrictionist, spoke for most reformers when he observed that "All the great problems, the liquor question, the public school question, the problems connected with prisons and reformatories and many more are tied up with the one great problem of immigration."[35] Thus, reformer and conservative, business and labor, redneck and social worker--virtually all Americans looked upon the immigrant as a phenomenon, a problem, a threat, but almost never a person.

Perhaps the credo of the reform generation was best capsulized by Brigadier General (LL.D.) Thomas M. Anderson. Replying to a questionnaire from the Immigration Restriction League, he asserted:

> I have learned that the essential thing in dealing with the discontented and submerged classes is to impress them with our disinterested honesty and to convince them that our Government will first use all means to conciliate and then all means to crush. The immigrant must be made to understand that a Republican Government can and will enforce its laws as despotically as a monarchy. . . . I favor stricter tests with races not assimilated with ours. I would like to exclude the Russians, Slavs, Asiatics, Greeks and Southern Italians. Northern Italians I consider desirable. Poles and Magyars are liberty loving and make splendid soldiers. So also do the Swedes, but I have found them inclined to socialism.[36]

---

[34] An insight into organized labor's reaction to the restriction question can be found in U.S. Immigration Commission, *Statements by Societies Interested in Immigration*, 61st Cong., 3rd Sess., 1910-1911, Senate Document 23; also Arthur Mann, "Gompers and the Irony of Racism," *Antioch Review*, XIII (Summer, 1953), pp. 203-14. Business' attitudes are explored in Morrell Heald, "Business Attitudes toward European Immigration 1880-1900," *Journal of Economic History*, XIII (July, 1953), pp. 290-304.

[35] Quoted in Solomon, *Ancestors and Immigrants*, p. 101.

[36] *Report of the Immigration Commission*, p. 120. This letter was one of over 100 from lists of *Who's Who in America* in response

The General, in a real sense, spoke for the American people. He also spoke for the reform groups here studied who believed democracy possible only in an atmosphere of cultural monism.

---

to Prescott Hall's questionnaire concerning their views on immigration restriction. According to Hall (p. 107) 375 favored further restrictions, 28 opposed, 307 favored literacy tests. Among those favoring further restriction were "presidents of 20 colleges or universities, 38 lawyers, 126 educators, 52 authors, 48 doctors, 29 clergymen, 21 Army and Navy Officers. . . ." Only 7 favored total restrictions reflecting the racial nature of their opposition.

CHAPTER II

SETTLEMENTS, CHARITIES, AND THE CULTURAL COLD WAR

> The prosperous classes have begun to find that a demoralizing political regime, bred in the midst of an alien, ill-favored way of life is getting its hold upon the affairs of their pleasant residential districts, and even at times threatens important downtown business interests.[1]
>
> Robert A. Woods
> South End House
> Boston

> [Immigrant institutions] meet their members needs . . . [and] manage to achieve a most interesting and worthy social type; but the result is not democracy in our terms.[2]
>
> Albert J. Kennedy
> Robert A. Woods
> South End House
> Boston

> [Immigrants lack] social energy which makes for progress . . . the inherent uncleanliness of their minds prevents many men from rising above the ranks of labor.[3]
>
> Jane Addams
> Hull House
> Chicago

---

[1] Robert A. Woods, ed., *Americans in Process* (Boston and New York: Houghton Mifflin, 1903), p. 358.

[2] Robert A. Woods and Albert J. Kennedy, *The Settlement Horizon - A National Estimate* (New York: Russell Sage Foundation, 1922), p. 328.

[3] Daniel Levine, *Varieties of Reform Thought* (Stephens Point, Wisconsin: Worzalla Publishing Company, 1964), p. 22.

[A] settlement might do charity work, although when the word "charity" is mentioned the settlement usually shivers as though its mantle were a wet blanket.[4]

      Julia C. Lathrop
      Hull House, Chicago

For three years the bureau [charities] was in almost constant contact with this family and through the services of a friendly visitor and other means made every effort to induce or compel this man to do his duty in the home. During this period two children died. The family was in abject want, the children without shoes, no fire, no food, and the man idle and indifferent. While anxious to prevent further suffering to the wife and children, we felt unable consistently to give physical aid to any extent . . . because of the attitude of the husband; and we decided that he must be forced to work or be sent to jail.[5]

      Bleeker Van Wagenen, President
      New Jersey Charities

We have about five million foreign-born voters in this country. Now who are going to give the standards. . . . Are you and I who understand and revere American institutions and who want to see these foreign-born voters conform to the same ideals which we hold?[6]

      Warren C. Eberle
      Field Secretary
      North American Civic
      League for Immigrants

---

 [4]Julia C. Lathrop, "What Settlement Work Stands For," *Proceedings of the Twenty Third Annual Meeting of the National Conference of Charities and Corrections 1896* (Boston and London: George H. Ellis Company, 1896), p. 108 (hereafter cited as *N.C.C.C.*).

 [5]"Minutes and Discussion," *Twenty Ninth N.C.C.C. 1902*, pp. 378-79.

 [6]Testimony of Warren C. Eberle, *Proceedings of the Thirteenth New York State Conference of Charities and Corrections 1913* (Albany: J. B. Lyon Company, 1913), pp. 113-14 (hereafter cited as *N.Y.C.C.C.*).

During the early years of the twentieth century, charity organizations and settlements began the subtle transformation into what is today called professional social work, a movement generated by the growing complexities of urbanization, industrialization, and ethnic diversity. Despite their eventual merger into a single profession, the origins, purpose, and methods of charities and settlements were distinct and often antagonistic. The advocates of each approached the other with much suspicion and not a little calumny. University bred for the most part, settlement workers viewed charity workers with condescension and even contempt. In their opinion, charity organizations were too narrow in approach and purpose, intruded upon the poor and the ethnic minorities, and were overly burdened with administration and bureaucracy. To the charity worker, on the other hand, settlements were often dominated by intellectual condescension, administrative chaos and too close an affinity to radical people and radical ideas.

Both settlement and charity workers however, were quick to criticize in each other faults which they failed to see in themselves. They allowed their superficial differences to obscure their more essential common characteristics. One such characteristic was their common origin. Historians have traditionally traced settlements and charities to English predecessors and have explained their development in the United States in terms of urbanization and industrialization.[7] This interpretation is, at best, only partially correct because it ignores the most essential feature both had in common. A factor unique to the United States and which provided much of the motive force and framework for both settlements and charities was the cultural and institutional confrontation between white, upper-middle class, Protestant Americans and the millions of immigrants who were often not so white, not so Protestant and definitely not middle class. The ensuing clash catapulted the charity and settlement movements into the front lines of the cultural cold war. In the process of demanding conformity to their own culture, they ordered in effect, the demise of all others. As both settlement and charity workers understood it, "victory" in this cultural

---

[7] Among the traditional accounts of settlements and charities are the following: Amos G. Warner, Stuart A. Queen, and Ernest B. Harper, *American Charities and Social Work* (New York: Thomas Y. Crowell and Company, 1919); Frank D. Watson, *The Charity Organization Movement in the United States* (New York: Macmillan, 1922); Robert H. Bremner, *From the Depths* (New York: New York University Press, 1956); Jane Addams, *Twenty Years at Hull House* (New York: Macmillan, 1911); Woods and Kennedy, *The Settlement Horizon;* and William I. Cole, *Motives and Results of the Settlement Movement,* Publication No. 2 (Cambridge: Harvard Department of Social Ethics, 1908). Three recent works which also discuss industrial and European origins are: Alan Davis, *Spearheads for Reform* (New York: Oxford Press, 1967); Roy Lubove, *The Professional Altruist* (Cambridge: Harvard University Press, 1965); and Kathleen Woodroofe, *From Charity to Social Work* (Toronto: University of Toronto Press, 1966).

confrontation was the achievement of a cultural monism in which the immigrant hordes surrendered their distinctive traits, accepted middle class values, and patterned their institutions on the American example. The clash between the invading ethnic cultures and that already established in the United States provided a crucial ingredient to the development of both the settlement and charity movements.

Until recently, historians have ignored this central feature of settlement and charity work. They have emphasized the English origins of the two movements, the emergence of social work as a profession, or the role of settlements in the reform movements of the progressive era.[8] The explanation is readily apparent. In the first place, ethnic and immigration history is of relatively recent vintage. Historians of progressivism have been far more interested, until lately, with overall political and economic accomplishments than with the interrelationship between progressives and ethnic minorities. Moreover, the nature of charity and settlement work has immunized it, to a large extent, from unfriendly criticism. Charity and settlement workers have acquired among historians a martyr's image. After all, the social workers gave generously of their time, effort, and often money to work among those less fortunate than themselves. Some, like Jane Addams and Lillian Wald, dedicated their whole lives to bringing about their versions of a more just and more humane social order. In the process, they gave up the ease and comfort of womanhood in upper middle class society and lived among the poor and deprived. Historians of the period have found far more likely candidates for criticism.

The charges and countercharges with which settlements and charities bombarded each other often broke into public view. One settlement worker, F. B. Peabody, succinctly presented the settlement critique before a convention of the *National Conference of Charities and Corrections (N.C.C.C.)*. "There can hardly be anything more opposed to conventional charity than the social settlement," he thundered:

---

[8] Examples of some of the new criticism of the progressive era in general are Levine, *Varieties of Reform Thought;* Gabriel Kolko, *The Triumph of Conservativism* (New York: Free Press of Glencoe, 1963); and Robert H. Wiebe, *The Search for Order 1877-1920* (New York: Hill and Wang, 1967). A more sympathetic view of the immigrant has evolved from such studies as: Oscar Handlin, *Race and Nationality in American Life* (Boston: Little, Brown, 1957); *Immigration as a Factor in American Life* (Englewood Cliffs, N.J.: Prentice Hall, 1959); *The Uprooted* (Boston: Little, Brown, 1951); Barbara Solomon, *Ancestors and Immigrants* (Cambridge: Harvard University Press, 1956); Roger Daniels, *The Politics of Prejudice* (Gloucester, Massachusetts: Peter Smith, 1962); and John Higham, *Strangers in the Land* (New Brunswick, New Jersey: Rutgers University Press, 1955). A fine analysis critical of Jane Addams and by implication the settlement movement can be found in Levine, *Varieties of Reform Thought,* Chapter I and Christopher Lasch, *The New Radicalism in America 1889-1963* (New York: Alfred A. Knopf, 1967), Chapter I.

> Its representatives have an almost morbid terror
> of being involved in charity. . . . The settle-
> ment workers live among the poor, and their rela-
> tion with them is that of neighbors and personal
> friends. They dismiss altogether the notion of
> social classes. They recognize but one social
> circle--the comprehensive circle of human sym-
> pathy and need.

Peabody closed his attack by characterizing the charity approach as little more than "philanthropic condescension."[9]

Settlement workers believed that their superior training enabled them to avoid the condescension and patronization so common among charity volunteers. Thus, while the charity workers remained interlopers, settlement workers thought themselves an integral part of the immigrant community. Mary McDowell of Hull House explained this point to an audience of charity workers as follows:

> The settlement is necessarily a work going on
> from within . . . the charity organization
> with its voluntary friendly visitors and its
> paid agents who must keep an exact record
> of all cases is the force from without coming
> into the neighborhood.

Julia Lathrop, McDowell's colleague from Hull House, added that charities were too narrow in outlook and purpose. They were concerned only with superficial problems among ethnic minorities. Settlement workers, on the other hand, she boasted, "are trained to look for causes [of social ills] . . . and are earnest to find the roots of the matter."[10] The superior education of the settlement workers--in their own eyes-- somehow made them a genuine friend of the immigrant and able too to attack his fundamental problems.

The settlements also objected to the short-sightedness of charity workers. Jane Addams once administered such a tongue lashing to the *N.C.C.C.* on this score that she later had to soothe hurt feelings with the cleverly worded apology, "we have always been anxious to avoid the affectation of saying that the settlement is superior to

---

[9] F. B. Peabody, "Social Settlements," *Twenty Fourth N.C.C.C. 1897*, p. 329.

[10] Julia Lathrop, "What Settlement Work Stands For," *Twenty Third N.C.C.C. 1896*, pp. 108-09. Mary McDowell, "The Settlement and Organized Charity," *Ibid.*, p. 124. For an interesting evaluation of the conflicting intellectual origins of the charity and settlement movements see Robert Hunter, "Relations Between Social Settlements and Charity Organizations," *Twenty Ninth N.C.C.C. 1902*, pp. 302-14.

charities."¹¹ The gist of her criticism had been that charity workers interpreted poverty only in terms of pauperism. She claimed that, much like prison authorities, charity workers were anxious to be rid of their charge, to restore the dependent to self reliance and then abandon him. In contrast, Addams asserted that the settlements worked for the restructuring of the urban-industrial social order. By maintaining its relationship with the alien and the derelict for prolonged periods, the settlement was able to "adjust the individual to civilization as he finds it round him, to . . . induce him to push up that civilization a little higher--not thinking . . . that he may lose something of his own caste and standing in the process. . . ."¹²

Yet in this address, Jane Addams revealed herself to be guilty of the same condescension as those whom she accused. She remarked that the "intellectual outlook" of the immigrants was "so narrow that lectures on only a few questions really interest them, because their senses are so dulled and tired, only music with a real swing or sensuous appeal interests them much." Elsewhere she explained her task was to "lead them out into something fine, world wide and awakening."¹³ Had Jane Addams scrutinized her settlement movement as meticulously as she did the charities, she would have discovered many similarities.

If settlement workers were hostile towards charity workers, the feeling was certainly mutual. Since many charity organizations were religiously affiliated, they were deeply critical of the lack of religious emphasis in the settlements. Charity workers found particularly threatening the settlement's emphasis on "a whole new moral order." In addition, many charity workers sympathized with the common accusation that settlements were hotbeds of radicalism. One charity representative

---

¹¹"Minutes and Discussion," *Twenty Fourth N.C.C.C. 1897*, p. 475.

¹²Peabody, "Social Settlements," *ibid.*, p. 339. Apparently, the strained relations between settlements and charities continued until well after World War I. Writing in 1922, Woods and Kennedy, *The Settlement Horizon*, pp. 190-91 claimed that they limited cooperation with charity organizations to dealing with paupers only so that the settlement could "avoid distraction from its educational and comprehensive purpose." Mary Simkhovitch, founder of Greenwich House in New York City, also criticized the shortcomings of charities. "We had seen the charitable approach to social problems and found it wanting. If social improvements are to be undertaken by one class on behalf of another, no permanent changes are likely to be affected. The participation by all concerned is necessary." *Neighborhood* (New York: W. W. Norton Company, 1938), p. 93.

¹³Peabody, "Social Settlements," *ibid.*, pp. 339-42.

bluntly asserted that settlements were breeding grounds for "single tax and all manner of isms . . . [and] extreme opinions." He was willing to concede, however, that this could be good if the radicals could be convinced by "people who think along other lines."[14]

In retrospect, the settlements' assessment of the shortcomings of the charity approach was sound, the counter charges less so. The animosity which the charity organizations engendered among the immigrants was a harsh reality with which the settlements had to contend. Two of Boston's South End House residents hinted at the extent of this hostility when they wrote "the intensity and universality of this recoil [against charity workers] give it a peculiar hold upon the settlement mind."[15] The charity approach, as its record of accomplishments demonstrates, certainly deserved critical reappraisal.

The charity movement in the United States was heavily indebted intellectually to the Manchester school of rugged individualism which so deeply permeated nineteenth-century British economic thought. This school equated economic success with righteousness, diligence, and thrift. Poverty, on the other hand, indicated a lack of virtue and worth. Thus, the Manchester school held that deprivation and decadence were causally related. In other words, it bolstered the deep-rooted American puritan ethic. Operating on these basic assumptions, the charity workers most concerned themselves with the negative task of stamping out pauperism.[16] Thus, to the charity worker, people who had jobs exhibited the glorious virtue of self reliance and were no longer the concern of charity. On the other hand, the best way to handle paupers was to instill in them the zeal to work.

The settlement workers were appalled at the narrowness--and often brutality--of the charity approach. Mary Simkhovitch, the founder of Greenwich House in New York City, proposed in 1908 that the charity organizations should cooperate with her in case work studies of the many immigrants just above the poverty line. Her proposal met with rude rejection. The charity spokesmen objected that the indigent "must put up with intrusion for their own good but the better-off should be shielded." Mrs. Simkhovitch argued in vain that case work, properly handled, was not intrusion at all. She argued for a broader definition of poverty and its related problems. She correctly perceived that charity workers interpreted their job as intrusion because they saw

---

[14]Lathrop, "What Settlement Work Stands For," *Twenty-Third N.C.C.C. 1896*, p. 110. "Minutes and Discussion" *Twenty-Fourth N.C.C.C. 1897*, p. 473. Davis, *Spearheads for Reform*, pp. 110-12. Mary Simkhovitch, "The Casework Plan," *Thirty-Sixth N.C.C.C. 1909*, pp. 137-49.

[15]Woods and Kennedy, *The Settlement Horizon*, p. 192.

[16]Hunter, "Relations Between Settlements and Charities," *Twenty-Ninth N.C.C.C. 1902*, pp. 302-04.

charity as a rather unpleasant means of urging people to be self reliant. In short, the more unpleasant it was to deal with charity, the more intense would be the recipient's desire to avoid it.[17]

The obsession to instill rugged individualism into their clients often blinded charity workers to the brutality of their failure to act. In New Jersey, for example, for three years the Orange County Bureau of Charities refused to give aid to a family because the father would not work. As the charity worker involved described the case:

> For three years the bureau [charities] was in almost constant contact with this family and through the services of a friendly visitor and other means made every effort to induce or compel this man to do his duty in the home. During this period two children died. The family was in abject want, the children without shoes, no fire, no food, and the man idle and indifferent. While anxious to prevent further suffering to the wife and children, we felt unable consistently to give physical aid to any extent . . . because of the attitude of the husband; and we decided that he must be forced to work or be sent to jail.

Eventually, the mother and yet a third child died of disease and malnutrition.[18] One charity worker bragged that in Toledo, Ohio, charity organizations handled deserters by having them "arrested and sent to the stone yard and made to work." He boasted that the wife received 40¢ a day.[19] Another asserted before the National Conference of Charities and Corrections that the best way to force a husband to work was to refuse aid to the family and thus increase its suffering. In the discussion which followed all but one speaker agreed that it would be unwise to aid a family unless the husband was helping to support them.[20]

---

[17]Simkhovitch, "The Casework Plan," *Thirty-Sixth N.C.C.C. 1909*, pp. 142-44. Many articles written by charity workers suggested the dominance of the puritan ethic. Particularly useful and pertinent is *Charities* journal during the period and other citations in this section. An excellent example of Charities deep felt fear of immigrants is provided in Charles Loring Brace, *The Dangerous Classes of New York and Twenty Years Among Them* (New York: Wyncoop and Hallenbeck, 1872), pp. 74-76 and 446-47.

[18]See footnote 5.

[19]"Minutes and Discussion," *Twenty-Ninth N.C.C.C. 1902*, p. 378.

[20]*Ibid.*, pp. 378-85. Statement by S. C. Lowenstein, Federation of Jewish Charities, Cincinnati, Ohio.

The charity worker was limited by more than his zeal for self reliance, however. In fact, self reliance was but one characteristic of the cultural heritage he was fighting to defend. He saw his country inundated by hosts of foreigners whose ways "strained if not subverted" his "noble heritage." Thus, one speaker at the National Conference of Charities and Corrections asserted that all patriotic Americans must "set in motion forces designed to conserve the heritage bequeathed us by our fathers."[21]

The fear of cultural mongrelization was central in the charity worker's mind and it at once made the immigrant problem important and blinded charities to the deeper causes of social ills. The result was, that as the twentieth century dawned, charity workers, with mounting fear, began to interpret most social problems in terms of "Americanism" versus "foreign influence."

An excellent way to illustrate the predominance of the cultural clash is to compare the charity worker's description of social problems with his assessment of their causes or implications. For example, in 1909, Sarah W. Moore, superintendent of Camp Schools, Society for Italian Immigrants, gave the following eye witness account of the horrors of mining camp life for the immigrant:

> The ordinary labor camp has little cheer; mud ankle deep, beer kegs and refuse at every corner; darkness unrelieved except for the flitting lantern; a place of toil, danger, separation, broken fragments of families, human kind crowded together in shanties furnished exclusively with bunks and possibly a table [for which the immigrant had to pay]; no spot to put apart the sick or even the dead; no Sunday rest, no weekday rest except the rainy day; a host of bewildered strangers practically mute and bereft of speech in a strange land.

One might have readily expected Miss Moore to have followed this tragic description of human exploitation with a rousing call for mining safety reform, health and sanitation improvement, humane working hours or living wage. Instead, her primary concern was that these immigrants were not being exposed to "the ways of Americans" particularly while they were "still plastic and responsive to wholesome influence."[22]

---

[21] Peter Roberts, "Night Schools," *Thirty-Sixth N.C.C.C. 1909*, p. 233.

[22] Sarah W. Moore, "Labor Camp Schools" *Thirty-Sixth N.C.C.C. 1909*, pp. 236-38. Miss Moore was the superintendent of camp schools for the Society for Italian Immigrants, New York City.

From a concern to mold plastic foreigners to the ways of Americans, it was but a short step to blame social ills on foreigners. Fred F. Bauer, chairman of the Bureau of Dependent Children, Department of Public Charities, New York City, claimed that the major cause of dependent children was the "indiscriminate dumping of foreign paupers" in this country for whom lack of care for their children was "a disease which is infectuous." His analysis deterred him from examining the impact of ghetto subsistance on family life, the strain of prolonged unemployment or the tearing asunder of old world familial cohesiveness by new world values. Bauer's solution to the problem of dependent children was frightening. He suggested that the federal government establish a "corps of examiners" to keep immigrants under constant observation and investigation for three years after their arrival in the United States. This incessant surveillance would deter family disintegration. He further suggested that desertion be made a felony punishable by one year in the penitentiary at hard labor.[23]

Another charity worker, A. A. Bradley of Boston Associated Charities, provided an eyewitness account of Italian immigrant conditions in a Pennsylvania mining camp:

> They are huddled together in small rooms containing crude wooden bunks, ideal breeding places for loathesome disease. . . . [A sheriff's raiding party discovered] a building large enough to accommodate an American family of six or eight. The police found in it fifty Italians massed together . . . twenty others in the cellar lying naked in the straw, sleeping head to feet like so many hogs. The company houses are often decent buildings though extremely plain and rent from four to six dollars per month.

Like Sarah Moore, Bradley failed to ask why the company did not build more and adequate housing and proper facilities. Instead, he found the

---

[23]"Care of Dependent Children," *Charities*, VII (November 2, 1901), p. 371. A frightening solution to the tramp problem was advocated by Edmund Kelly in *The Elimination of the Tramp* (New York: Putnam and Sons, 1908). He suggested that the states most affected should erect concentration camps for their internment. Robert W. Hebberd, Commissioner of the New York City Department of Public Charities, wrote in a forward to the book, "The establishment by the state of an involuntary labor colony on wasteland susceptible of reclamation . . . should be recognized as a pressing necessity," p. V. R. Fulton Cutting, in a second forward endorsed the proposal so long as the produce of the tramp colony could be sold, "without interfering with private business or competing in the general market," p. IX. Kelly himself pointed out that railroads killed thousands of tramps annually. His main regret was that burial costs were too burdensome on the companys, pp. 7-11.

conditions he described as proof that the new immigrants were "beaten men from beaten races representing the worst failures in the struggle for existence." He also supported a hysterical resolution of the Boston Associated Charities which asserted that the "ignorant and foreign" represented a threat to "public morality" and rapidly became "helpless victims of the corrupt boss or of irresponsible agitators" and thus contributed to "the growth of the most dangerous form of anarchy and lawlessness."[24]

In retrospect, the settlement workers' indictment of the charity movement was generally sound. The charity approach was condescending, generated hostility among the immigrants, and therefore was unable to build any viable relationship with the disadvantaged. The limitations engendered by the charity outlook often prolonged suffering and human exploitation in the cause of fostering an Anglo-Saxon version of rugged individualism. Furthermore, the mounting hysteria over immigration predisposed many charity workers to interpret social ills in terms of a cultural confrontation. Thus, the charity movement was generally unable to evaluate critically the much more serious sickness at the heart of the urban industrial chaos. Yet while the settlements quickly discovered other's shortcomings, they were not so perceptive of their own.

Generally, the settlements shared many of the faults of the charity organizations. The settlement approach too was often condescending and elitist, but at the same time it was more subtle. The racism of the settlement workers was usually less overt than charity's. But, settlement workers were not so much the "insider" and the confidant of the immigrant as they imagined. The settlement worker dedicated himself to imposing upon the immigrant the values, manners, and institutions of his heritage. Because the leaders of the settlement movement developed a penetrating understanding of economic, political and social problems, they were able to propose reform programs of a far reaching nature.[25] Yet, precisely because they constructed a broad blueprint for a new social order, they represented a serious threat to the cultural and institutional integrity of the immigrant. The monolithic

---

[24] A. A. Bradley, "To What Extent Does Unrestricted Immigration Counteract the Influence of Our Educational and Charitable Work," *Charities*, VIII (April 5, 1902), pp. 325-30. W. Almond Gates, secretary of the California Board of Charities and Corrections, presented an equally alarmist view of Chinese immigration which he accused, among other crimes and dangers, of, "sapping the manhood of the lower strata of the white race." Gates imagined himself involved in a "contest for supremacy" with the "wifeless, childless, yellow man." "Oriental Immigration on the Pacific Coast," *Thirty-Sixth N.C.C.C. 1909*, pp. 230-32.

[25] The comprehensive interests of the settlement movement as well as its affinity to political activism is discussed at length in Davis, *Spearheads for Reform*.

order espoused by the settlement leader, rejected out-of-hand most cultural characteristics of the ethnic minorities. Rather than build their new order around indigenous immigrant institutions, the settlements undertook a subtle kind of cultural imperialism.

Central to the settlement worker's attitude toward the immigrant was his paternalism. The headworker of East Side House of New York City epitomized this arrogance when he asserted that a major problem of the settlement was:

> How to reach a class of men of criminal or semi criminal tendencies and instincts and to hold them until . . . better things [were] substituted. The solution clearly did not lie . . . in making a direct appeal to the individual or spiritual nature of these men. That would have been to speak to ears which do not hear.[26]

This patronization severely limited the contact between the settlement and the immigrant. For example, East Side House restricted its social engagements, particularly the Monday night dance, to those small number of immigrants whose manners, morals, and demeanor coincided with those of the white upper middle class. When the dance had been open to all, the headworker complained, "the result was a mob of visitors, most of whom were strangers to us. So also were many of their customs. They did not comport with any established code of manners known to those in authority. . . . Democracy proved itself absolutely unable to rise to the level of the situation." In this case, the immigrants had shown themselves eager to cooperate with the American settlement worker but were rejected. After the immigrants were properly screened, the headworker was pleased to report, "The Monday night dance now is the occasion of innocent pleasure and enjoyed by all who frequent it. General decorum is marked and withal the best of fellowship obtains."[27] Outside this decorum, the "mobs" of "strangers" looked elsewhere for a helping hand and social outlet.

The headworker provided a significant insight into the elitist workings of East Side House in his 1905 report. Although the social events remained stringently screened, the headworker had inaugurated an attempt to allow the immigrants more voice in the operations of the house. He complained though of being greatly hampered by "the contemporaneous existence of a board of managers [which included Cornelius Vanderbuilt, J. P. Morgan, and George F. Crane], a contributing public, a large number of more or less order-loving people,

---

[26] New York East Side House, "1904 Report," *Reports 1892-1909* (New York: privately printed, n.d.), p. 8 (hereafter cited as *Reports*).

[27] *Ibid.*, pp. 10-11.

and a headworker with nerves."[28]

The condescension of the East Side House workers was by no means uncharacteristic of the attitude of most settlement workers. Robert A. Woods of Boston's South End House thought that immigrants were "barbarians" who must be imbued with "truly civilized conceptions of politics or of life in general."[29] Vida Scudder of Boston's Denison House referred to Italians as "the poorer people, mostly of the peasant class" whom she wanted to "relate to the life of cultured America."[30] Jane Addams complained of the immigrant's "inherent uncleanliness of mind." On several occasions she referred to their "primitivie habits" which she longed to uplift to American ways "which represented a distinctly superior standard of life and thought."[31] Even while defending certain aspects of immigrant culture (in this case parades and folk festivals) Addams could not conceal her feeling of superiority. "Nor is this display altogether gaudy," she observed, "it is full of charm and reminiscence, a great historic pageant which they themselves apparently do not yet understand."[32] Settlement workers were hardly immune from the cultural nationalism of their era.

---

[28] East Side House, *Reports*, 1905, p. 15. This passage raises interesting questions concerning the settlement house's sources of financial support and the influence of the benefactors in formulating policy. There is no study of the relationship between the settlement leadership and its sources of financial backing. Who the benefactors were and the conditions under which they made their funds available remains unexplored.

[29] Woods, *Americans in Process*, p. 150.

[30] Barbara Solomon, *Ancestors and Immigrants* (Cambridge: Harvard University Press, 1956), p. 165. In her chapter "Testing the Races: Stereotypes of the Foreign Born," Solomon correctly asserts that settlement workers were in the mainstream of racist and elitist thought in America. She also perceptively assesses the impact of those precious few settlement leaders who resisted racism and condescension. They were a "distinguished minority," but "unheeded," p. 176.

[31] Levine, *Varieties of Reform Thought*, pp. 22-23.

[32] "Report of the Committee," *Thirty-Sixth N.C.C.C. 1909*, p. 214. Interestingly, Jane Addams brought Jeremiah Jenks to speak to this conference of charity workers on the topic, "The Racial Problem in Immigration." Among the immigrant characteristics which Jenks attributed to racial inheritance were "readiness to assimilate, fecundity, overcrowding and crime, inclination to educate their young, economic business efficiency, and ability to promote the welfare of this country," pp. 215-22.

At times, the contempt they felt toward the immigrant caused the settlement leaders, like their charity counterparts, to ignore the results of their own investigations into the roots of immigrant misery. Robert A. Woods, for example, described in poignant terms the lot of the unemployed immigrant and his frantic efforts to avoid charity and to remain self sufficient. He explained that the immigrant exhausted his meager savings, sought credit at small basement stores, hunted jobs no matter how small or temporary, pressed his wife and children into work if necessary, and depended on relatives and friends who "often go to surprising lengths in supplying food and loaning money." He described the depressing and precarious plight of the immigrant working on the labor gang, traveling, who knew where, in search of work. In short, Woods most vividly portrayed a people who exemplified to the limits of human endurance the virtues of industriousness, thrift and self reliance. Yet the conclusion he drew from his study was no different than his contemptuous pre-suppositions. He contended that for all their tribulations and misery, immigrants could blame no one but themselves. Because of the "low standard of wages and expenditure which . . . [they] bring with them," he insisted, "the newcomer remains an enemy to all that is best in American life and cannot expect to be received into the friendly fellowship of American citizens." He went on to express regret that, "subsidies of charitable relief are unfortunately more available than resources in the way of self support."[33] Woods was far closer than he would have admitted to the attitude of the charity bureaucrat who espoused prolonged suffering for the poor in order to encourage self reliance.

Much of the condescension of the settlement worker had racial undertones. For example, Frederick Bushee of South End House complained that Jews were "deficient in civic sense" and that Italians were "much more docile" than other races.[34] Two of Bushee's fellow residents concluded that the cause of overcrowding among Jewish immigrants was "their inborn love of money-making."[35] Even Jane Addams lamented that the intellectual inferiority of the southern Italian made him much more difficult to reach than the "superior educated Teutonic guests."[36] This racist attitude toward the immigrant

---

[33] Woods, *Americans in Process*, pp. 129-46.

[34] Frederick Bushee, "The Invading Host" in *ibid.*, p. 70. See Davis, *Spearheads for Reform*, p. 102, who rightly asserts that most settlements were swept up in the "racist hysteria" of the age.

[35] Jessie Beale and Anne Withington, "Life's Amenities" in Woods, *Americans in Process*, p. 239.

[36] Jane Addams, *Twenty Years at Hull House* (New York: Macmillan, 1911), p. 235.

manifested itself in the formation of derogatory stereotypes of the newer immigrant nationalities. These vague generalizations neatly bolstered the settlement's ass-mption of its own cultural superiority.

The settlement's persistent emphasis on the superiority of the native culture may have been a subtle defense mechanism against the gnawing fear that American culture was shallow and vulnerable to foreign influence. In a remarkable passage in *The Settlement Horizon*, Woods and Kennedy admitted to the dread of settlement workers being assimilated into alien ways rather than vice-versa. They grieved over the number of settlement houses:

> In which the residents became more or less assimilated to the standards of the immigrant group or groups about it. It is, of course, among the risks of propaganda that the propagandists shall himself suffer conversion. Occasional residents take on the more showy personal qualities of certain European types, adopt less rigid standards with respect to personal relations than those of our own country, and incline towards an internationalism based on indiscriminate mixture of peoples. The fact that a few houses are overcolored by cosmopolitanism is an indication of the eifficulties overcome by the successful majority.[37]

This passage is revealing in several respects. First, it shows that the indoctrination process to which the settlements exposed the immigrants--presumably concerning the cultural worth of the various immigrant traditions and values--was little more than "propaganda." In fact, the settlement worker considered his task to be the dissemination of propaganda. Some settlement leaders were alarmed that a few of their co-workers really acted in accord with the proposition that the immigrants were worthy in their own terms. Second, the passage exposed the repugnance of the majority of settlement workers to developing any personal or intimate ties with the immigrant groups. Finally, it makes abundantly clear that assimilation was to be a one

---

[37] Woods and Kennedy, *The Settlement Horizon*, p. 331. The above was taken from a chapter appropriately entitled "Race and Place." Woods and Kennedy clearly saw Americanization as a one-way process. They declared that their primary task "is to impart American standards and ideals . . . and to assist them in adjusting their life to ours. . . . Americanization is an evolution into national fellowship through mastery of our standard of living and of life," p. 326. At another point, the authors expressed apprehension that unless the settlement worker were exceptionally dedicated to Americanism he ran the risk of being "carried away by the oftimes stronger native [immigrant] force of natural leaders among boys and girls of the neighborhood," p. 428.

way process. "Internationalism" and "cosmopolitanism" were pitfalls which the superior American avoided at all costs.

There has been considerable scholarly research into the subjective motivation of settlement workers. A prevalent interpretation holds that since the settlement workers were upper-middle class, well-educated, and exposed to social and economic ills, they were disgusted with the uselessness of the life which their culture demanded of them.[38] Jane Addams, for example, complained bitterly that the upper class values from which she fled produced wasted lives, "as pitiful as the other great mass of destitute lives." She added that upper class Christian women "hear constantly of the great social maladjustment, but no way is provided for them to change it, and their uselessness hangs about them heavily . . . they are sustaining the shock of inaction."[39] In other words, many social workers fled to the settlements from a culture which they considered decadent and which condemned them to lives of listless leisure. The confrontation with the multi-cultured immigrants forced them to defend cultural values which they themselves had begun to doubt. The settlement workers, as Woods and Kennedy testified, were acutely aware of the weakness and shallowness of their own values. This sense of cultural vulnerability probably sharpened the settlement worker's fear of succumbing to foreign influence.

Because the settlement workers' fear of foreign inundation was buttressed by their own self doubts, they, like their counterparts in charity work, embarked upon a program of cultural attrition. The best defense of their vulnerable American values was to neutralize or destroy those values and institutions which threatened them. Woods and Kennedy succinctly warned that the challenge of the settlement was "to impart American standards and ideals . . . and to assist them [the immigrants] in adjusting their life to ours."[40] Jane Addams apparently agreed that the major problem in dealing with the new immigrant was to make him conform to American standards. In fact, a primary objection she had to the segregation of the Negro (Hull House had established a separate branch for black people) was that it "tends, in itself, to put him [the Negro] outside the immediate action of that imperceptible but powerful social control which influences the rest of the population."[41] For the preservation of Americanism, it was very

---

[38] See Lasch, *The New Radicalism in America*, Chapter I. Also Davis, *Spearheads for Reform*, "The Settlement Impulse."

[39] Addams, *Twenty Years*, pp. 20-21.

[40] Woods and Kennedy, *The Settlement Horizon*, p. 326.

[41] Jane Addams, *The Second Twenty Years at Hull House* (New York: Macmillan, 1930), p. 396.

important that no foreign ethnic values or institutions be allowed to prosper outside the "social control" of the defenders of the faith.

In the quest for cultural conformity, the settlements often worked against viable immigrant cultural and institutional establishments. Indigenous immigrant aid societies, political organizations, and certain cultural relationships such as close family cohesiveness, often obstructed the progress of settlement infiltration. Most settlement workers were not concerned with the effectiveness or serviceability of immigrant institutions, but rather with their conformity to upper-middle class standards. In fact, to the settlement leadership, immigrant institutions were dangerous in direct proportion to their effectiveness. Woods and Kennedy clearly feared that the immigrants were establishing viable institutions. "Immigrants work and earn their living," they warned:

> Under the direction of other immigrants, and their institutions are in charge of leaders born and trained abroad. The children frequently go to schools taught by young people of foreign-born households [in the parochial schools], who . . . have never mastered the genius of English speech . . . [and] have no adequate knowledge of the customs, manners, and subtle nuances of ideas and ideals that make the real spirit of the nation . . . [immigrant institutions] *meet their members needs* . . . but the result is not democracy in our terms. [Consequently] there is a certain crossing of purposes between the settlement . . . and many forms of racial organization.[42] [Italics mine]

Thus, the settlements, willing to accept the immigrants only on their terms, chose to combat immigrant efforts to help themselves, rather than to cooperate with them.

In the effort to condemn immigrant ways, the settlement groups sometimes judged foreigners by standards which Americans themselves did not meet. For example, Woods and Kennedy asserted that immigrant families did not exhibit "the understanding between teacher and parent which characterizes the normal American community at its best. . . . Only when a boy or girl so far outraged order that punishment was demanded was father or mother summoned to interview teacher or principal." For this reason the immigrants were accused of "creating a tradition inimical to American standards."[43]

---

[42]Woods and Kennedy, *The Settlement Horizon*, pp. 327-29.

[43]*Ibid.*, pp. 274-75. The inclination to find fault with immigrant habits caught the authors in obvious inconsistencies. For example, they accused the Irish of the inability to recognize that "difficulties might be overcome by common action," yet they later

In effect, Woods and Kennedy compared the interest of immigrant parents toward the American education system with the "best" of the American community—that is, those American parents who actively participated in educational affairs. A more interesting comparison might have emerged had Woods and Kennedy studied the intensity of interest among average Americans in their school system. They probably would have found that most Americans then, as now, took an interest in their son's school only when his disciplinary problems or the "racial situation" compelled them.

Probably the most solidly entrenched immigrant institution and the one which provided the ethnic minorities with the most services and amenities was the political machine. Yet, partly because of the bosses' corruption and partly because they exhibited standards which "represented the extreme step in setting aside our American precedents,"[44] the settlements opposed the boss and all that he stood for.

The settlement worker understood well the services rendered by the ward healer. Robert Woods, for example, wrote a superb analysis of the political boss' role in immigrant life. The ward politician, he perceptively observed:

> Must see that his poor families' rent is paid;
> he must secure legal assistance for the oppressed
> immigrant; he has to arbitrate legal disputes; he
> must secure for the sick admission to the hospital;
> he is pressed to use his best endeavors to get am-
> bitious but incapable girls into high or normal
> school; he must find places for them as steno-
> graphers or teachers when they have finished their
> education; he must put the poor, worthy and un-
> worthy alike, in the way of receiving help from

---

enviously admitted that the "Celtic element molded sentiment and controlled local politics and residents. . . ." p. 332. In the same paragraph, they accused the Jewish immigrants of "lack of inclination toward local public spirit" yet admitted that "Jews are carrying the spirit of [community] service into their work as teachers, lawyers, doctors and public officials," p. 333.

[44]Woods, "Traffic in Citizenship" in Woods, *Americans in Process*, p. 154. Davis, *Spearheads for Reform* indicates the extent of the settlement's political maneuverings against the ward bosses. Davis' account of the conflict is only partly true. He assumes that the charges against the bosses were valid simply because the settlement workers made them. Yet at no point does Davis indicate the existence or extent of the deep rooted cultural animosity which makes more understandable the popularity of the ward healer among their immigrant constituents. The cultural conflict also clarifies the immigrant's resistance to the public school system.

>church or municipal charities; he is beseiged for
>opportunities for work by widows and helpless people.
>He makes it his business to defend the culprit be-
>fore the law, advancing bail, securing witnesses,
>getting the complaint smoothed down, the penalty
>eased. . . . He is certainly human in the variety,
>the universality of his interests and service.

Thus, Woods had described the urban immigrant ward healer as a provider of the services and amenities which were necessary for survival in America's hostile urban environment. Yet, even while admitting the enormous worth of the boss to the immigrants, Woods could not refrain from commenting, "As a philanthropist under enlightened standards he could hardly pass, still he is inclined to believe himself one."[45]

To the immigrants, the boss was not only a dispenser of goods and services. He was also the protector of their cultural and institutional heritage. The boss' most frequent boast was his closeness to his people. One ward healer bragged of his strong support of a bill making it mandatory that neglected children be boarded out to families of the same faith. He thus defended his people from what they saw as a threat from Protestant America. He voted for relaxation of drinking restrictions on the Sabbath, and thus struck a blow against the American tea drinkers. He worked for the abolition of dark cellars and the death penalty because he saw that his people were so often their victims.[46] In this sense, the boss was a kind of front line defender of the immigrant in what both perceived to be the cultural onslaught of Anglo-Saxondom.

Thus the settlements singled out the bosses as special targets in their reform programs. Jane Addams, for example, carried on a relentless campaign against boss Johnny Powers between 1894 and 1898. She accused him, among other things, of being against education for the immigrant children of the ward. Yet, while Powers used his influence to thwart the efforts of Hull House to build another public school in his district, he was not against education for his immigrant constituents. He was working hard to build another parochial school in the neighborhood. Thus, the issue was what kind of education his immigrants would receive. The parochial school not only educated, but it protected and perpetuated the religious and cultural heritage of the ethnic minorities. In short, the confrontation between Addams and Powers was, in part, a manifestation of cultural conflict.[47]

---

[45] *Ibid.*

[46] *Ibid.*, pp. 152-54. See also Samuel P. Hays, "The Politics of Reform in Municipal Government in the Progressive Era," *Pacific Northwest Quarterly*, LV (October, 1964), pp. 157-69.

[47] Davis, *Spearheads for Reform*, pp. 152-62.

Despite Addams' utmost efforts to defeat Powers in the 1896 election, he won by a much larger margin than he had two years earlier. Powers scoffed at the settlement workers when the campaign ended. "I may not be the sort of man the reformers like," he boasted, "but I am what my people like, and neither Hull House nor all the reformers in town can turn them against me."[48] Powers was obviously right. The settlement group, contrary to their claims to intimacy with the immigrant, were not "insiders" at all. To most immigrants they represented an effort to impose, from without, strange institutions and new molds.

The writings of the settlement workers themselves suggest that they were not as close to the immigrants as they thought. Jane Addams complained of her inability to establish "genuine relations" with Italians. The headworker of East Side House confessed that "the house is doing only a small portion of the work it ought to do. It has not yet taken its rightful place in the community." Woods and Kennedy ruefully observed the "smoulderings of distrust . . . and an occasional outbreak of active prejudice" against the settlements. Mary Simkhovitch revealed one important reason for the distrust. She explained that her Greenwich House workers attempted not only to be "in" with the immigrants, but also to act as funnels of information to the city authorities. In fact, one of the residents was the city tenement house inspector, who, "taught us how to keep on the watch for violations as we went in and out of neighbors' homes." But the distrust and suspicion were manifestations of deeper hostilities. While trying to adjust to American life, the immigrant tried desperately to preserve something of his own. The settlements demanded that with the possible exception of "immigrants gifts" in which they allowed him pride, the immigrant must be made over in a new image.[49]

The immigrants also had good reason to be suspicious of settlement activities in education. Johnny Powers attempted to alleviate the well-founded fears of his community when he favored a parochial instead of a public school. The settlements offered education and kindergarten programs of their own, pressured city schools for special efforts in immigrant education, and even advocated carefully selected reading programs. All of these efforts had one end in common—to transform the immigrant into the settlement's image.

Helen Moore of the New York University Settlement, for example, sponsored a systematic reading program for the immigrants. Her

---

[48]*Ibid.*, p. 162. For a fascinating and sympathetic portrayal of a ward healer and his relationship with his people see Hutchins Hapgood, *Types from City Streets* (New York: Funk and Wagnalls, 1910), pp. 56-74.

[49]Addams, *Twenty Years*, p. 235. East Side House, *Reports*, 1908, p. 11. Woods and Kennedy, *The Settlement Horizon*, p. 167. Simkhovitch, *Neighborhood*, p. 101.

goal was not to awaken critical minds, but to create complacent ones. She tailored her program for "the child of foreign parents, who in the first blush of patriotism, inspired by the school flag, is burning with a desire to know something of United States history . . . the right kind of wholesome, joyous books that shall bring sweetness and light into their lives, and ideals of virtue and civic duty into their minds." But Moore did not desire to foster "civic duty" only. She also eliminated books which "takes them [the immigrants] into the rich man's parlor and shows only luxury and elegance."[50] To this settlement worker, as well as to many others, education was meant to feed the immigrant a steady diet of sweetness, joy, and patriotism and to hide from him the more critical perspective which might reveal the depth and the cause of his misery.

The settlements sought to indoctrinate the immigrant in every phase of their education program. Even kindergarten was designed, in the words of one worker, to superimpose upon the immigrant the values of a "good home" which included "habits of punctuality, regularity, industry, obedience, respect for the rights [read property] of others . . . [and] a regard for law and order."[51]

The settlements also provided hefty portions of indoctrination in the "civic duty" courses which practically all of them offered.[52] The overall purpose of these classes was to "develop the desired qualities of hand, mind, or morals in the particular class or nationality or age group with which it works."[53] But to many immigrants it was clear that the qualities to be instilled were desired, if not demanded, by the settlements rather than the immigrant. Furthermore, the qualities on which the settlement workers seemed to put a premium were complacency and docility. The settlements attempted to produce a human product which would be as pliable and uncritical as possible.

One well-educated immigrant participant described a similar Americanization class at the YMCA in the following terms:

---

[50] W. Frank Persons, "Readings for the Poor," *Charities*, VIII (May 3, 1902), pp. 419-20.

[51] East Side House, *Reports*, 1908, p. 12.

[52] Katherine B. Davis, "Civic Service of Social Settlements," *Twenty-Third N.C.C.C. 1896*, p. 133. Davis presented a chart which showed that of twenty-two settlements answering her inquiry, only three did not offer such courses. The goal of "civic duty" training was to inculcate "character, honesty, integrity and manhood and womanhood that will make civic corruption impossible," p. 137. The implication was clear that immigrants lacked these qualities.

[53] Woods and Kennedy, *The Settlement Horizon*, p. 163.

> [I] was appalled at what I saw. Not only were the
> teachers utterly ignorant of the language of the
> men they taught . . . [Italian] but they were
> completely out of touch with the educated elements
> of the immigrant communities. The contents of the
> textbooks in use exhorted the workers to love and
> honor the boss and to obey the foreman as if he
> were Jehovah himself. It was the sort of humiliating
> tripe which was bound to alienate any workman with
> a trace of character and independence.[54]

Settlement workers made little effort to seek out immigrants of character or independence. Instead, in their dealings with the public schools, the settlements sought to capitalize on what they understood to be the naiveté of immigrants. Two public school coordinators from South End House described in glowing terms the transformation of the immigrant child which they had the honor to help bring about:

> Certainly the change which comes over children is a
> swift and apparently spontaneous one. A little girl
> of foreign birth and stammering tongue . . . tells
> an English visitor that the beautiful portrait of
> the Father of his Country . . . is Buffalo Bill.
> This is the beginning. A few grades higher a group
> of boys of foreign birth are celebrating Washington's
> birthday. In mimic scene they reproduce the pro-
> ceedings of the First Continental Congress, states-
> man after statesman answering as his name is called.
> The gentleman from Virginia delivers . . . his great
> utterances, hardly able to await his turn, the
> gentleman from Pennsylvania protests in vain. At
> last all agree vehemently to hang together or hang
> separately and they affix their names to an imaginary
> Declaration of Independence, their audience cheering
> the while with excitement and joining with the
> patriots later in singing fervently and unquestioningly
> 'Land where our fathers died.'[55]

While the public education system was directly responsible for this particular exercise in political indoctrination, the settlement workers wholeheartedly approved it and used their influence to establish other such special classes for immigrants.

---

[54] Norbert Wiener, *Ex Prodigy: My Childhood and Youth* (New York: Simon and Schuster, 1953), p. 267.

[55] Caroline S. Atherton and Elizabeth Y. Rutan, "The Child of the Stranger," in Woods, *Americans in Process*, pp. 317-18.

However, the influence of the settlement on the public schools was not entirely a manifestation of the demand for cultural conformity. Indeed the settlement workers were in the vanguard of those who pressured for industrial education, free lunch programs, accelerated English courses and the like.[56] Yet the settlements were also in the advance eschelons of those who saw education as little more than carefully programmed propaganda designed to remold the immigrant and convince him that the new mold was fitting.

A precious few settlement workers denounced political indoctrination and the quest for cultural homogeneity. Lillian Wald of the House on Henry Street was one of a handful of settlement workers who scorned "surface patriotism." "Great is our loss," Wald predicted, "when a shallow Americanism is accepted by the newly arrived immigrants, more particularly by the children, and their national traditions and heroes are ruthlessly pushed aside." Speaking as much to the contemporary ethnic crisis as to her own era, Wald condemned the reluctance of Americans to accept the immigrant except on their own terms. With compassion and insight rare among her fellow settlement workers, and rarer still among Americans in general, Wald boldly challenged her countrymen to reassess their prejudices:

> It is difficult to find evidence of any serious effort on our part to comprehend the mental reactions upon immigrants of the American institutions he encounters. Indeed . . . I sometimes wonder if he . . . does not hold up a magic mirror wherein our social ethics are reflected. . . . What we are to the immigrant in our civic, social and ethical relations is quite as important as what he is to us. We risk destruction of the spirit--that element of life that makes it human--when we disregard our neighbor's personality.[57]

---

[56]*Ibid.*, pp. 295-96. The authors were instrumental in having showers installed in one of the public schools heavily attended by immigrant children. The teachers administered six hundred showers per week. See also Davis, *Spearheads for Reform*, "The Settlement and Education" and Lawrence Cremin, *The Transformation of the Schools* (New York: Alfred A. Knopf, 1959), Chapter III.

[57]Lillian Wald, *The House on Henry Street* (New York: Henry Holt and Company, 1915), pp. 302-04. Among her colleagues, only a very few such as Emily Balch and Mary Simkhovitch shared Wald's favorable attitude toward cultural pluralism. These few, along with those whom Woods accused of "internationalism" were closer intellectually to the radicals of the era than they were to their settlement colleagues. This group of free spirits which included Mabel Dodge, Emma Goldman, Hutchins Hapgood and "Big Bill" Haywood is

However humane, Lillian Wald was also unrepresentative of settlement or charity thought. To the teeming hordes of ghetto-dwelling immigrants, both represented a serious threat to cultural ties with the old world. Desperately trying to adjust to his new home, the immigrant soon discovered that settlements and charities would help him only if he relinquished his past sense of cultural identity and assumed a new one which they deemed more acceptable.

In retrospect, charity and settlement workers were classic examples of the environmental theories which they so fervently espoused. They reflected--sometimes in spite of themselves--the values and fears of their era. Their intellectual and cultural milieu was molded by alarmist predictions of race suicide, general acceptance of Anglo-Saxon supremacy, and rising protest against ethnic minorities. Their society was beset by Jim Crow, lynching bees, and imperialism. In such an atmosphere, settlements and charities hardly could have done other than they did. Their dominant attitudes were America's. Despite their conflicting self-images, settlements and charities stood side by side in the front ranks of the cultural cold warriors. Both joined forces with those ardent defenders of American civilization, the educators, who found their classrooms glutted with armies of the great unwashed.

---

discussed tantalizingly by Henry May, *The End of American Innocence* (New York: Alfred A. Knopf, 1959), pp. 302-32. See also Lasch, *The New Radicalism in America, passim*. For an example of the sympathetic approach of one of this group toward the immigrant see Hutchins Hapgood, *The Spirit of the Ghetto* (Cambridge: Harvard University Press, 1967) and his *Types from City Streets* (New York: Funk and Wagnalls, 1910).

CHAPTER III

EDUCATORS, IMMIGRANTS, AND THE RISE OF INDUSTRIAL EDUCATION

"The instructors [Santa Fe Apprentice School] exercise a modified military and parental discipline over the boys; the military discipline will insure immediate obedience and subordination; the parental discipline will assure the boys of the personal interest taken in them and serve to teach them the importance of becoming an honest citizen."[1]

"When in the school printshop the boys nudge each other and whisper, 'Gee, this is just the way they do it down town'. . . . It is this idealized view of the industrial world which I seek to take advantage of in the earlier years of the elementary school in laying the foundation for future citizenship. . . . [This naiveté provides] a splendid basis for the philosophy of both life and of industry."[2]

"The New York high school stands ready to ally itself with the dominant interests in any town and to give vocational

---

[1] F. W. Thomas, "Educating Apprentices on the Santa Fe," *Proceedings of the National Society for the Promotion of Industrial Education*, Bulletin No. 13, Part II (New York, 1911), p. 65 (hereafter cited as *N.S.P.I.E. Proceedings.*)

[2] S. J. Vaughan, "The Moral Significance of the Vocational Motive," *Education*, XXXIII (June, 1913), pp. 596-97.

instruction demanded by such interests. . . ."[3]

The champions of the cause of industrial education, though not as publicized as the settlements and charities, were every bit as energetic, influential, and organized in waging their version of the cultural cold war. In theory, industrial education was supposed to rescue urban education from its doldrums by making it relevant to the new industrial era. Many progressives supposed vocational education to be among the noblest of means in the quest for efficiency, order, and increased productivity. Yet industrial education touched the lives of the foreign high school student or apprentice workman in a way that was often oppressive, misguided, and had little to do with education. Industrial training instilled in the immigrant new cultural values, tried to create a docile and uncritical work force, and delayed the time when a worker might expect skilled wages. Industrial education became an instrument in the reculturalization of the immigrant because of the nature of the industrial-educational alliance which promoted it.

A number of forces compelled business leaders to embrace the industrial education movement. In the first place, their own apprentice programs were ill-attended, produced few graduates, and were difficult to staff. Businesses were unable to train enough workers to man their increasingly complex machinery. Second, the enormous numbers of foreign born workers were particularly hard to train because of language barriers. This problem in turn deterred plant efficiency and increased safety hazards. Third, many business executives, particularly in times of labor unrest and agitation, saw the need to give the unschooled immigrant worker a proper dose of anti-radical instruction. Industrial education seemed to answer all these needs. It trained workers to meet the increased skills demanded by industry at taxpayers expense. The program also taught immigrants English and in the process inculcated those habits of promptness, docility, and obedience which industry expected of its employees. And, industrial education instilled in the foreign workers not only love of America and its corporate system, but also suspicion of those who criticized either.

Pressures of a different nature led educators to align themselves with businessmen. Many educators saw industrial education as a means of making education relevant to the new industrial era. In the sense that industrial education was training for life, many considered it to be in the mainstream of progressive educational innovation. For others, industrial education provided an ideal answer to the problem of what to do with the immigrant child. Many educators felt that immigrants were culturally and intellectually inferior to Anglo-Saxons and were therefore incapable of appreciating or performing

---

[3] New York State Assembly, Department of Education, *Ninth Annual Report, 1913*, 136th Sess., Vol. XII, No. 26, Part I, p. 128.

well in traditional academic disciplines. For those with little mental capacity, educators asked, could not America at least train them to use their fingers? Furthermore, many educators felt keenly the need to Americanize foreigners. Industrial education provided the framework within which the immigrant could be persuaded to trade foreign heroes and values for American ones. Needless to say, the teachers with the lowest opinion of immigrants also saw in industrial education a means of segregating the less fit and of preventing them from contaminating the children of good Anglo-Saxon stock or from diluting the quality of their education.[4]

Thus, for different reasons, educators and industrialists found themselves promoting the same cause. The education-industrial alliance which that cause forged became a formidable political pressure group at the state and national level and, in many industrial communities, also dominated the local school system.

The lobby and chief organ of the education-industrial alliance was the National Society for the Promotion of Industrial Education, founded in Boston in 1907. One year later, the *N.S.P.I.E.* had established chapters in eight states and lobby committees in twenty-nine others. The board of managers of the national organization was comprised of twenty-five members. Seven were educators by profession, twelve were industrialists, five were involved in some aspect of social work and one represented the royalty of the skilled labor movement, the Brotherhood of Electrical Workers. The first elected officers were Henry S. Pritchett (president of Carnegie Foundation), president; Everett Macy (chairman of the Board of Trustees, Teacher's College, New York), treasurer; M. W. Alexander (General Electric Company), vice-president; and C. R. Richard (director of Coopers Union), secretary.[5] Of the sixteen officers listed for the eight state branches, eight were industrialists and eight were educators. At least one-third of the membership were industrialists or educators.[6]

At the federal level, the *N.S.P.I.E.* was influential in promoting national aid to vocational education. In 1909, President

---

[4] The attitudes of industrial leaders as well as educators will be examined in detail in this and subsequent chapters.

[5] *N.S.P.I.E. Proceedings*, Bulletin No. 1 (New York, 1907), p. 6.

[6] *N.S.P.I.E. Proceedings*, Bulletin No. 7 (New York, 1908), pp. 25-26. This bulletin also lists the national membership of approximately one thousand. Of these, about three hundred fifty are listed by title. Practically all of these were affiliated either with educational institutions or industries. The publications of the *N.S.P.I.E.* are valuable sources of the opinion and practices of labor, education, and business groups in the field of industrial education.

William Howard Taft appointed two of the society's prominent members to the commission on National Aid to Vocational Education. The commission's recommendations were virtually written into law with the passage of the Smith-Hughes Act of 1917.[7]

At the state and local level the educational industrial coalition campaigned for vocational courses at the high school level and promoted innovation and experimentation in industrial education. Most of the experiments were locally controlled and were designed to meet the particular training requirements of nearby factories. Among the boldest and most universally praised of these experiments in industrial education was the co-op school. The co-op school, as its name suggested, was a public school which cooperated closely with local industry in the formulation, control, and staffing of its industrial education program. The public school excused participating pupils to work as apprentices in local factories usually on a half-time basis. In addition, the course work in the industrial education program was altered by the addition of special courses, many taught by local business executives or plant foremen. Other special courses were designed to implant in the student (who was usually foreign born or second generation immigrant) an uncritical love of country and an enthusiasm for the status quo of the corporate system.

Within three years of the founding of the N.S.P.I.E., thirteen co-op schools were established in industrial centers, mostly in the east.[8] Two of the most famous of the co-ops were the Beverly School in Beverly, Massachusetts and the Fitchburg Industrial Co-op in neighboring Fitchburg, Massachusetts. The inner workings of these two highly acclaimed schools provide an interesting perspective on the education-industrial alliance.

The Beverly School, almost from its inception in 1909, was one of the darlings of educational reformers. Perhaps the co-op concept was so enthusiastically received by educators because of their

---

[7] U.S., Congress, House of Representatives, *Report of the Commission on National Aid to Vocational Education*, 63d Cong., 2d Sess., 1914, House Document 1004, p. 1. Hereafter cited as *Vocational Aid Commission Report*. Of the five non-congressmen named to the commission, Charles A. Prosser and Florence Marshall belonged to the N.S.P.I.E. The four congressmen who completed the commission were Senator Hoke Smith, Georgia; Senator Carroll S. Page, Vermont; Representative D. M. Hughes, Georgia; and Representative S. D. Fess, Ohio. Smith and Hughes sponsored the legislation for national aid to vocational education which eventually became law. Senator Page had offered similar legislation earlier. Thus, at least five members of the nine man commission were publically committed to a national program of vocational education.

[8] U.S., Commissioner of Labor, *Industrial Education*, 1910, Twenty-Fifth Annual Report of the Commission of Labor, pp. 187-99.

basic agreement with industry's point of view. The director of industrial training at Fitchburg High School, for example, was most sympathetic to industrial problems. "The employer has to take these misguided and ill-trained products [of the high school] into his employ," he complained, "and at a tremendous economic loss, give him a post graduate course in real live business methods and processes."[9] To the many educators who agreed, the Beverly School and others like it offered ideal solutions. One educator proudly proclaimed that those pupils privileged to attend the Beverly School "have constantly here before them as an object lesson the great factory conducted under the most ideal conditions." The commission on National Aid to Vocational Education concurred by asserting that the Beverly School provided, "the ideal democratic education . . . [where students acquire] the ability to live happy useful lives as citizens of a democracy." Speaking for an important segment of progressive reformers, Jane Addams, herself an active member of the N.S.P.I.E., enthusiastically endorsed and promoted the co-op movement. She described the co-op school as, "A most significant experiment in the direction of correlating the schools with actual industry . . . whereby boys . . . are thus intelligently conducted into the complicated process of modern industry."[10] Despite the enthusiasm of many progressives and educators, a closer examination of the Beverly School would have revealed that among those students who enrolled, few lived happy lives, and fewer still learned much about the rights and responsibilities of citizenship in a democracy.

    The Union Shoe Company was the primary industrial employer in Beverly. In 1910, the shoe company employed one-quarter of the total population of 18,650--that is, between three and four thousand persons. In 1909, asserting that "community industrial-education must be based on community industrial interest,"[11] M. B. Craven, general superintendent of the Union Shoe Company, founded the Beverly School. Working closely with city and state educational authorities, Craven combined the resources and staff of the local high school and the Union Shoe Company. True to Craven's principle, the Beverly School had one capability and one purpose only--to train shoe machinists.[12]

---

[9] *N.S.P.I.E. Proceedings*, Bulletin No. 13 (New York, 1911), p. 128.

[10] Waldo Frank, "The Beverly Factory Industrial School Plan," *Education*, XXXV (March, 1915), p. 443. *Vocational Aid Commission Report*, p. 95. Jane Addams, *Twenty Years at Hull House* (New York: Macmillan, 1911), p. 440.

[11] Frank, "Beverly School Plan," p. 434.

[12] *N.S.P.I.E. Proceedings*, Bulletin No. 13, Part III (New York, 1911), p. 116.

A student enrolling in the Beverly plan could not be certified as a skilled machinist or qualify for skilled pay, unless he completed the full four year course. Instead of the normal nine month school year, Beverly students (those enrolled in the industrial program only) "attended" fifty weeks which they equally divided between the high school and the Union Shoe Company. The students worked twenty-five weeks of fifty work hours each in the factory. They spent the other twenty-five weeks attending classes at the high school on a normal thirty hour per week basis. However, the students devoted half of their school time, fifteen hours per week, to industrial oriented courses taught by machinists from the shoe company. According to the terms of the contract between the company, the local school board, and the state, the Union Shoe Company provided and paid the machinist instructors in the factory and the classroom and also furnished the raw materials and the machinery. The company kept all its own accounts of maintenance costs which were reimbursed through state and local taxes. These costs included "power, light, heat, and rental of floor space and machinery." The company further agreed to buy all the student-made shoes which passed inspection (that is which could be sold at retail on the open market) at "an established price."[13] One need hardly observe that under the contract state and local taxpayers paid the Union Shoe Company's power, light, heat, and even machinery depreciation costs. Or more precisely, taxes paid whatever share of those expenses the company, in its own audit, claimed as legitimate.

Such losses as the company might have incurred through incomplete reimbursement (which probably never occurred) were easily recovered through the Beverly School wage system. The company paid the first year apprentice-student a wage of seven cents per hour. A second and third year student received nine cents per hour.[14] A fourth year student's salary was negotiable. The exceptional machinist might even make a full skilled salary of twenty-nine cents per hour.[15] Thus under the stated wage scale, the company was guaranteed three years of labor from the Beverly students at roughly one-quarter the wages it would have had to pay other machinists. The company in addition withheld one-half of its wages to Beverly students to further defray "operating costs."

In his laudatory article in *Education*, Dr. Waldo Frank revealed that the average weekly salary for a first year apprentice was $7.35 but only $3.75 net. He further stated that by the end of his third year the student had raised his net income to $4.35 per week--an increase of sixty cents per week. But Frank made no further

---

[13] *Ibid.*

[14] Frank, "Beverly School Plan," p. 441.

[15] *Vocational Aid Commission Report*, p. 96.

comment on why there was a fifty percent difference between gross and net wages.[16] The statistics quoted by the commission on National Aid to Vocational Education substantiated Frank's figures on net wages The commission reported that the average hourly wage for first year students was 4.3 cents, rather than the 7 cents per hour claimed by Frank. The mystery of the disappearing half was solved by A. L. Safford, a former superintendent of the Beverly School, in testimony before the N.S.P.I.E. He admitted that half of the wages were returned to the company to "pay the difference in cost between maintaining the school job and any other similar job in the factory."[17] In other words, not only did the state and local authorities pay the company for "overhead," but the students returned one half of their wages toward the same end. In addition, the company made at least normal profits from all the shoes which it purchased from the students at "established prices."

But the company found still other ways to supplement its profits through its experiment in co-op education. The company had agreed to provide and pay the machinist instructors at the school. Yet the records of the state of Massachusetts raise serious doubt about who was paying the instructors' salaries. The records list the Beverly School as having four teachers.[18] Actually, the company paid for only two who received thirty to thirty-five dollars per week or at least twice the average wage for machinist work. This meant that on paper the company paid its two machinist instructors between $3000 and $3500

---

[16] Frank, "Beverly School Plan," p. 441.

[17] *Vocational Aid Commission Report*, Appendix C., p. 96. The statistics show that of the seventy-three enrollees in 1909, only twenty-two graduated four years later. The report also casts serious doubt on the claims of the Union Shoe Company that fourth-year students made a wage of 29¢ per hour. The company paid its full-time apprentices in the class of 1912, a total of $5,338.40. There were at least twenty-two full-time apprentices because that number graduated. Simple arithmetic shows that the 29¢ wage was more mythical than real--
29 x 22 = $6.38 (price per hour/per twenty-two students); $6.38 x 50 = $319.00 (price per twenty-two students/ per fifty hour work week); $319.00 x 50 = $8,075.00 (total wages which should have been paid for twenty-two students at an average rate of 29¢ per hour). Using a reverse process on the actual total wages paid ($5,338.40), discloses that the average hourly wage actually paid was not quite 19¢ per hour. Thus, even during the fourth year, when apprentices were supposed to be paid 29¢ per hour, they probably earned no more than two-thirds of that.

[18] Commonwealth of Massachusetts, Annual Reports of Various Public Officers and Institutions, *Education*, 1910, Vol. VIII, Doc. 2, p. 150 (hereafter cited as *Massachusetts Education Reports*).

per year. The other two instructors were employed part time--fifteen hours per week at a rate of $1.00 to $1.50 per hour. Their salaries were paid by the school board.[19] One might reasonably expect then, that because the company paid the two full-time instructors, the "overhead" of the Beverly School would be approximately $3000 to $3500 less than other industrial schools of comparable size employing two teachers. But such was not the case. Actually, the Beverly School cost state and local taxpayers as much as any industrial school of similar size employing *four* full-time instructors at state expense.[20] This suggests that either expenses at Beverly were exceptionally high or the company's expense account assured that even the instructor's salaries were reimbursed through "overhead costs."

But one need not have examined the Massachusetts records or studied the wage scale to see that there was something wrong at Beverly. When the former superintendent of Beverly, A. L. Safford, appeared before the N.S.P.I.E., his presentation reeked with the gloom and dissatisfaction with which the local populace greeted the Beverly School. But neither he, nor the co-op enthusiasts to whom he spoke, seemed to pay any attention.

Safford's entire speech was an ill-concealed defense against what was obviously a hostile local reaction. He began with the denial of the evidently often-heard charge that Beverly provided, "an excess of workmen to take the place of the present employees at a reduced wage." He further confessed that the Beverly School, "was not established in response to a strong popular demand and consequently is not yet strongly entrenched in popular favor. It has been received sympathetically on the whole . . . [yet] contrary to popular impression . . . it was [not] intended to benefit the manufacturer rather than the boys." The people of Beverly must have also accused the company of manipulating the high school curriculum because Safford exclaimed that the public school was, "of course conducted in a manner to receive their [Union Shoe Company] approval as a whole, though not necessarily in detail." He also defended the school against what must have been an embarrassing charge of indentured servitude because he compared Beverly to some corporation schools and concluded proudly that "In this school, there is no indenture. A pupil is free to leave at any time." Safford concluded on another ominous note:

> But we have our troubles. . . . The first great
> danger to the school is a certain amount of
> inertia and indifference on the part of the
> general public. If the school should "strike

---

[19] *N.S.P.I.E. Proceedings*, Bulletin No. 13 (New York, 1911), p. 116.

[20] *Massachusetts Education Reports*, 1910, p. 129. Comparative Statistical Table.

a snag" nobody knows what attitude the public
would take. Serious consequences might result
from the lack of the right kind of public support.
. . . The greatest difficulty of all has been to
secure suitable teachers. The two machinist
instructors were chosen from 3,500 employees of
the company and there were less than half a dozen
available that we felt that we could consider at
all.[21]

    This last admission was nothing short of astounding. The teachers earned between $30 and $35 per week which was more than twice as much as the average machinist's wage of 29¢ per hour. This rate was apparently competitive, because the certified graduates of the Fitchburg Industrial School earned, as full-time workers, "no less than two dollars per day" or twelve to fourteen dollars per week.[22] Either the most profound animosity or a most amazing concentration of incompetence accounted for only six of 3,500 being "available" for consideration to instruct at the Beverly School. What Safford chose to ignore, albeit uneasily, was the utter, undeniable unpopularity of his co-op plan among the workers and their families. It was plain to all except those who did not want to see, that the Beverly School was of, by, and for the Union Shoe Company. The company kept the accounts and was reimbursed by taxes for what it claimed were its expenses. The company sold the shoes the boys made for at least normal profit. The company raked off half of what was already an ungenerous wage scale, thus assuring itself of at least three years of almost wageless labor. The people of Beverly discovered early that the Beverly Plan was not in their interest.

    Another highly touted experiment in cooperation was the Fitchburg Plan. Under this plan the Fitchburg High School, Fitchburg, Massachusetts, cooperated with a number of local industries to provide training in various manual skills. For this reason, the school at Fitchburg was more flexible than the one at Beverly.[23] Nor did

---

    [21]*N.S.P.I.E. Proceedings*, Bulletin No. 13 (New York, 1911), pp. 111-122.

    [22]U.S., Bureau of Education, *The Fitchburg Plan of Industrial Education*, Bulletin No. 50, 1913, p. 28. Testimony presented by Matthew R. McCann, English High School, Worchester, Massachusetts (hereafter cited as *Bulletin No. 50*).

    [23]*N.S.P.I.E. Proceedings*, Bulletin No. 13 (New York, 1911), p. 96. Testimony of W. B. Hunter, director of the Industrial Department, Fitchburg High School. The manufacturers cooperating with the Fitchburg plan were: Simonds Manufacturing Company (saws and knives), Fitchburg Steam Engine Company, Bath Grinder Company (grinding machines),

Fitchburg deduct fifty percent of its wages for overhead costs.

Like Beverly, on the other hand, the Fitchburg industrial course was of four years' duration. The student spent his first year attending special classes in high school. The next three years, he alternated between shop and school. He worked every other week in the factory full time. The company contracted to pay the apprentice ten cents per hour the first year, eleven cents the second and twelve and one-half cents the third. According to the figures cited by the director of the school, the boys worked a fifty-five hour week.[24]

One of the most interesting aspects of the Fitchburg plan was the contract. Each student was required to sign a contract between himself, the company involved, and the student's parents or guardians. The contract bound the company to pay the student the wages specified for 1,650 hours per year. It also allowed the student two weeks vacation without pay during the summer, *but* there was no way for the student to take his vacation without losing time. Furthermore, all "lost time" had to be "made up before the expiration of each year at the rate of wages paid during that year, and no year of service shall commence till after all lost time . . . shall have been fully made up." In effect, the student was allowed no vacation at all. The contract was not clear as to whether the student had to work during Christmas and Easter vacations.[25] Apparently, the student's parents

---

Blake Steam Pump and Condenser Company, Cowdrey Machine Company (woodworking machinery), Putnam Machinery Company (general tools and machinery), Fitchburg Machinery Company, Brown Steam Engine Company, Jennison Company (tinsmithing and pipe engineering), and the Goodnow Company (iron works).

[24]*N.S.P.I.E. Proceedings*, Bulletin No. 13 (New York, 1911), p. 96. In this testimony, W. B. Hunter showed that at 10¢ per hour, a student earned $5.50 per week; at 11¢, $6.05 per week; and at 12.5¢, $6.87 per week. All three totals were obviously based on a fifty-five hour work week.

[25]U.S., Bureau of Education, *Bulletin No. 50*, p. 21. The bulletin shows that the student worked twenty-eight weeks of fifty-five hours each or 1,540 hours per year--*if* he took a two week vacation. This obviously left the boy 110 hours short of his contract or two full weeks. Thus the student could not take his contract-guaranteed two-week vacation without delaying the beginning of his next academic year. The only other alternatives were to forego the vacation altogether, or work a sixty hour work week (five hours overtime per week) throughout the entire year. See Appendix A-1, A-2, and A-3. These are reprints of the contracts in their entirety. The contract was vague as to whether the student was required to work during traditional school vacations such as Christmas or Easter, but apparently, the language could be construed to require such work. See clauses 3 and 4. All appendices are reprinted from *Bulletin No. 50*.

had to put up a one hundred dollar bond to assure the company that the boy would not break the contract. The commissioner of labor reported of the Fitchburg plan that, "By the terms of the indenture, the employer reserves the right to terminate the agreement when he sees fit, but if the boy quits he forfeits a bond of $100."[26] Thus the contract assured the company of 4,950 hours of work from each student at an average rate of 11¢ per hour over a three year period. Put another way, the businesses associated with the Fitchburg Plan paid each student about $550.00 for three years of work. This could not have been much more than the Union Shoe Company paid the students for their last three years of work.[27]

The students reported to the company thirty weeks per year for full-time duty. The authorities of the Fitchburg High School provided the youngsters with a list of "practical suggestions" to guide their relations with their employers. Among the more interesting were the following:

> Remember that the object of work is production. . . . If you get the mistaken idea that any work given you is beneath the dignity of a high school boy, just remember you are an apprentice and get 100 per cent busy. It is your business to get along smoothly with the workmen and foremen; not theirs to get along with you. Do not expect any personal attention from the superintendent. He will probably ignore you entirely, but he knows whether or not you are making good, and in most cases his idea of you depends upon your ability to please your foreman. Don't be a kicker and don't continually bother your foreman for higher wages. . . . Watch, in a quiet way, what things are being done

---

[26] U.S., Commissioner of Labor, *Industrial Education*, 1910, p. 188. The agreement was made between the parents of the student apprentice and the participating company. The high school was not a party to the contract, but acquiesed to the procedure. The contract allowed the company to suspend or relieve a student, "without previous notice."

[27] If Frank's figures were correct, the average gross wage for the second and third year at the Beverly School, was 9¢ per hour (4.5¢ net). Therefore, the average wage paid for the last three years at Beverly was 9.3¢ per hour or only 1.7¢ per hour less than the average wages paid under the Fitchburg plan. The arithmetic is simple once again to figure the average net wage for the last three years at Beverly. 4.5¢ (1st year) + 4.5¢ (2nd year) + 19¢ (3rd year--see footnote 17) = 28.0¢ ÷ 3 = 9.3¢.

around you, and don't be afraid to ask sensible
questions. A good rule is to think over a question
twice before asking. A reputation for having
"horse sense" means that you are making good.
Foremen and workmen will take pleasure in
showing you, if you show yourself genuinely appreciative of little attentions. If they tell
you something you already know, don't spoil
their pleasure by telling them you already know it,
but let it be impressed on your mind all the
deeper; for the conversation may lead to something
which is entirely new to you.
If your foreman refuses to grant any requests, and
you value his good will, do not refer the matter
to a higher official.[28]

But if the school gave the boys practical hints about how to get along as workers in the business world, the business leaders evidently helped to mold the high school educational program as well. The high school course for the co-op students was specifically designed to produce the "right attitude" in the workers. The English course, for example, was geared to the needs of the shop and toward instilling in the student an appreciation of the, "history of successful men." Included in the collateral readings for the freshman English course were such titles as the following: *Romance of Industry and Invention, Romance of Modern Electricity, Romance of Modern Manufacturing, Story of the Railroad,* and *Careers of Danger and Daring.* During the sophomore year, the students were required to write themes on "the description of shop tools etc." and to read, "mechanical journals and biographies of successful men." In the junior year, themes were assigned on such topics as, "Manufacturers of Fitchburg, The Steam Engine, and Railroads and Their Influence on Fitchburg." In addition, the student studied the "Autobiography of Franklin, Webster's Bunker Hill Address, Washington's Farewell Address and Lincoln's Addresses."[29] The commissioner of labor described the civics course, as, "a study of daily happenings in the industrial world, the history of the iron industry, the factory system, new inventions and the reading of mechanical journals."[30] No one could

---

[28] See Appendix A-4 for full document.

[29] U.S., Bureau of Education, *Bulletin No. 50*, pp. 17-18. See Appendix A-5.

[30] U.S., Commissioner of Labor, *Industrial Education*, 1910, p. 189.

honestly accuse the Fitchburg School of providing a well-rounded education.[31]

Whatever might have been the advantages of the Fitchburg Plan to the students, it was clear that the business community was the principal beneficiary. The manufacturers were not only guaranteed three years of cheap labor, but they were allowed to mold the education of the participants to the interests of the industrial community.

Yet the co-op movement did offer some real improvement over many of the corporation schools of the period. Many industries, in response to the demand for skilled machinists, had instituted apprentice systems of their own. These provided the precedent on which the co-op schools were patterned. Almost all of the corporation schools were at least four years in length during which time the employer found it lucrative to pay pitifully reduced wages and exert harsh discipline. Since most of the testimony bearing on the corporation schools emanates from the corporation spokesmen, any misjudgment in evaluating them would likely be on the side of generosity.

F. W. Thomas of the Santa Fe Railroad, for example, described the apprentice system of the railroad as a "splendid opportunity." The company required the apprentices to attend four hours of school per week for four years. The education was, "trimmed of all frills." For example, all fractions were taught in 64th, 32nd, 8ths, and 4ths because, "Mechanics in railroad shops have no use for 7ths, 9ths, or 13ths of inches. . . . Teaching a boy subjects foreign to his trade . . . tends to make his mind wander and oftentimes makes him dissatisfied with his vocation." The discipline in the school was harsh as Thomas' testimony suggested:

> The instructors exercise a modified military and parental discipline over the boys; the military discipline will insure immediate obedience and subordination; the parental discipline will assure the boys the personal interest taken in them and serve to teach them the importance of living a clean life and the value and importance of becoming an honest citizen.

Wages were exploitive. "Renumeration . . . is still too small. Many boys . . . accept positions which have practically no future to offer,

---

[31]Actually, the Fitchburg Industrial School probably over extended the duration of its course work no more than other industrial schools. The *Massachusetts Education Reports*, p. 144, described as follows the courses offered by the Boston Printing and Bookbinding School. "A four year course in printing, a four year course in printing and bookbinding, and a four year course in bookbinding and printing." The only four year course excluded was in bookbinding, and one guesses that the school was probably not far from inaugurating it.

but whose immediate gains are greater than that of the apprentice."[32]

George C. Cotton of the Solvay Process Company of Syracuse, New York, described his company's apprentice program. The four year apprentice course was mandatory and the company demanded that the student and his parents sign a contract certifying that all statements made on the application were true and that the parents, "request the Company to employ their son upon the terms agreed upon." Cotton did not specify the wages his company paid the apprentices, but he did indicate that the contract bound the company to nothing in particular. Between September 1909 and July 1911, thirty-seven boys enrolled, but only three graduated into the shops. Fourteen "dropped by the wayside"; six were "discharged" for "bad habits, quarrelsomeness and careless work"; and one "would not work."[33] If the company was so eager to eliminate apprentices before graduation, and if the program produced so few apprentices, one wonders why the company maintained the program. Perhaps the Solvay Company used its apprentice system as a means of ensuring labor at substandard wages.

The Fore River Shipbuilding Company of Quincy, Massachusetts, required an indenture contract which bound the worker to attend four hours per week, twenty-two weeks per year for four years. Wages were low enough that overtime was "very popular with the boys" because they were "allowed to do piecework and are given the difference between their regular wage per hour and their piecework earnings reduced 20%."[34] That meant that wages were so low that even when piecework was reduced 20% it paid enough over the apprentice rate to make overtime "very popular." This fact also suggested how badly underpaid the apprentices were in relation to their production value for the company.

One of the better, certainly one of the most applauded corporation schools, was established by Ludlow Manufacture Associates in Ludlow, Massachusetts. Joseph Eaton, director of the Yonkers Trade School described the school in glowing terms. He was particularly proud of the relationship between the company and the town which he related as follows:

---

[32]*N.S.P.I.E. Proceedings*, Bulletin No. 13, Part II (New York, 1911), pp. 62-68.

[33]*Ibid.*, pp. 76-81. For statements from company spokesmen, see U.S., Commissioner of Labor, *Industrial Education*, 1910, Chapter IV. The Solvay Company spokesman testified to the grim fact "School is in session fifty-two weeks per year," p. 180.

[34]U.S., Bureau of Education, *Industrial Education*, 1908, Bulletin No. 6, p. 33 (hereafter cited as *Bulletin No. 6)*.

> I propose to tell you about a small apprentice school which is supported and controlled by a prominent Massachusetts corporation. In order that this description may be fully understood, it will be necessary to make a few statements regarding the corporation itself and the peculiar relations which it bears to the town where it is located. The town of Ludlow, in which the school under discussion is situated, has about 5,000 inhabitants. By far the greater part of these are employed by the Ludlow Manufacturing Associates. . . . Practically all of the village of Ludlow is owned by the company. This means that nearly all of the taxes of the town are paid by this organization. Sewers are installed by men in its employ; parks are owned and maintained; streets lighted; and recreation and hospital buildings erected and partially supported by the Associates. The library building is a gift in memory of the former treasurer of the company. In fact "the company" and Ludlow are very closely related.
>
> Notwithstanding all this, all town matters and especially the public schools are entirely under the control of the townspeople. This class includes very few of the mill workers for, with scarcely an exception, the latter are foreign born. They are also but recent arrivals in this country and this statement may be applied to nearly all the mill foremen and superintendents as well. . . . The close relationship between town and company demands that this large foreign element must be "Americanized." So another important duty of the school is to give instruction in the duties and privileges of good citizenship. . . .
>
> Thus it may be seen that while the school aims at a definite mark, the target is rather large and a respectable score may be made even if it does not consist of any bull's-eyes.[35]

Charles W. Hubbard, the Treasurer of Ludlow Manufacture Associates, provided the philosophical impetus behind the school. In reply to a questionnaire sent out by N.S.P.I.E., Hubbard asserted that tax funds should be channeled into manual education rather than high school. He continued:

---

[35]*N.S.P.I.E. Proceedings*, Bulletin No. 10 (New York, 1911), pp. 100-01.

> I believe a large amount of money spent in the
> high school would be better spent in adding
> industrial training to the grammar schools, free
> education, whether intellectual, commercial or
> industrial should be given only to those who show
> distinct promise of becoming efficient workers
> in their chosen line. . . . [the others] should
> be dropped into the unskilled or obligated to
> get their education at the expense of their
> relatives and friends. . . . I believe that
> many who have received advanced schooling fail
> to repay the public for the expense of their
> education, and in some cases are injured by
> over education.[36]

Guided by this desire to produce "efficient workers" whose docility was ensured by their escaping the dangers of "over education," the Ludlow School tailored its courses to meet exactly the needs of its industry. Eaton described the school's approach to academic subjects without embarrassment.

> Thus far the mill has dominated the school work
> . . . and the so-called book work. Hence one
> may find in the list of studies such subjects
> as arithmetic, algebra and geometry, history,
> mechanics and English. . . . But most trained
> teachers would hardly recognize them as they
> are taught to our boys.[37]

Hubbard evidently won the battle against too much education.

Like all of the other co-op or corporation schools, Ludlow stretched its course into a four year program for which it paid an hourly wage of 8¢, 9¢, and 10¢ to 12¢ for the first three years respectively.[38] The industrial education movement was clearly exploitive.

---

[36] *N.S.P.I.E. Proceedings*, Bulletin No. 3 (New York, 1907), p. 27.

[37] *N.S.P.I.E. Proceedings*, Bulletin No. 10 (New York, 1911), p. 103.

[38] U.S. Commissioner of Labor, *Industrial Education*, p. 257. Wages for the fourth year were not mentioned. A question yet unanswered is why industrial schools were of four years duration. A New York Central Railroad official testified that "A student can be taught, on the average, to turn out 7/8 of the mechanics output after three or four days." U.S. Bureau of Education, *Bulletin No. 6*, p. 38. Yet the N.Y.C. RR. operated a four year mechanics course. In marked contrast, some of the philanthropic industrial schools such as the

Students or apprentices worked for a small fraction of their worth to the company. In some cases they were literally indentured by contract and under bond to industry. The academic education provided for the participants in the industrial program was carefully planned indoctrination. The co-op programs exploited the public as well. Their taxes supported the schools for whatever expenses local industry claimed. In the case of Beverly, there was strong evidence that the Union Shoe Company received considerably more from taxpayers and students than its actual expenses warranted. Yet Beverly, Fitchburg, and the rest won almost exuberant acclaim from the educators. The faults of the system went uncriticized, perhaps even unnoticed. Educators were, in fact, willing partners in the industrial education alliance.

To the teachers of the early twentieth century, the arrival of masses of immigrants must have presented an upsetting and exasperating challenge. The educator saw in his classroom every day the faltering of time-worn moralisms and trite patriotic maxims. The immigrant child's eyes did not light up properly when he heard the words of Patrick Henry. While the teacher expostulated on the evils of taking in boarders, the Italian boy wondered if his father had found a job. And so the educator, sure that Armageddon was impending, chose to re-enforce rather than re-examine his beleaguered maxims.

Perhaps more than any other profession, teachers saw themselves as the defenders of the faith. Into their hands was entrusted the heritage, values, and culture of the land, and theirs was the task of transmitting these intact--perhaps even a little embellished--to the next generation. So long as the new generation rose from the same stuff as the old, this task was not so difficult. But with the coming of the great unwashed of Europe, teachers realized that never again would their sacred trust be an easy one and yet never before had it ever been so crucial.

The educational journals and the reports of the state departments of education fairly bristle with a sense of impending doom. Kelly Miller, the noted Negro scholar, delivered a bitter indictment against the failure of education to cope with the problem of moral decay.

> Our jails and penitentiarys are full. Crimes
> against persons and property grows faster than

Baron Van Hirsch Trade School in New York City graduated qualified skilled workers after only 5-1/2 months. One motive for the extended duration of the course work was that it brought with it an extended supply of sub-paid workers. From the educator's point of view, a long vocational training period served to lengthen the period of "Americanization" for the foreign boys who participated. It also kept the juveniles off the streets until they were more likely to be employable.

> the population. Corruption taunts our municipal governments and graft flaunts our national politics. Selfishness, which today is expressed in the greed for gain, has penetrated our national life from the lowest to the highest places. Hatred of class against class is stimulated, crime in its most hideous as well as in its more recondite forms abounds. Education surely makes men wiser and more efficient, but it does not make them better.

Yet, when asked for a solution, Miller could do little more than suggest an appropriate homily, "A boy with blackened boots is apt to stay out of the mud."[39] Nathan C. Shaeffer, superintendent of Public Instruction for Pennsylvania, shared Miller's sense of doom. He thought that the influx of immigrants into the mining towns of Pennsylvania threatened not only morality, but America's political institutions as well. He claimed that the task of education was to "safeguard against the overthrow of our institutions by the enemies of freedom." Thus, education must "enforce the great truths which lie at the foundation of our civic and ethical life."[40] Shaeffer vigorously defended a 1913 state law requiring Bible reading in the schools as necessary, "for the sake of ethical instruction and moral uplift." Those "agnostics and atheists" who had constitutional qualms about the law, "should resign."[41] Edward Stitt, district superintendent of the New York City public schools, also felt a deep sense of foreboding. He was particularly alarmed by the problem of assimilating large numbers of unworthies into the American mainstream. "Coming as the pupils do," Stitt complained, "from homes of destitution, and not having been baptized with the Republican Spirit of New England, can we expect great results? There is a vast difference between the descendents of the Mayflower and the denizens of Mulberry Street."[42] Wherever the educator looked, he sensed that his education and his country were plunging headlong into a disaster of uncertain proportions.

---

[39] Kelly Miller, "Moral Pedagogy," *Education*, XXXIV (November, 1913), pp. 138-39.

[40] State of Pennsylvania, *Annual Report of the Superintendent of Public Instruction*, 1914, pp. 15-16.

[41] *Ibid.*, 1913, pp. 3-4.

[42] State of New York, Department of Education, *Ninth Annual Report*, 1913, 136th Sess., Vol. XII, Part I, p. 28.

And yet, all was not lost. The same superintendent who decried the denizens of Mulberry Street predicted in the next breath that a bold and rigorous program could save the schools, American political institutions and even the immigrant. He assured the fearful that:

> With wise leadership and progressive pedagogy to direct our forces we shall have every hope for the future that our alien boys . . . [will] become faithful citizens who love our public school system, who shall honor our flag and who shall ever rejoice in the permanency of American institutions.[43]

Perhaps implicit in the foreboding which permeated educational thought was a sense of urgency--the belief that only by an immediate and concentrated effort, tragedy could be averted and even the immigrant could be made to defer to the superiority of Anglo-Saxon judgment.

Prodded by this sense of urgency, the educators of the early twentieth century inaugurated many new programs designed to promote moral, political and cultural conformity in the immigrant. Teachers traveled to the coal mining regions to establish classes for the immigrant work gangs. They began to teach sex hygiene classes to remind students of the proper relationship between the sexes. Perhaps most widespread was the emergence of immigration classes within the public school system to teach the foreigner the English language and the Anglo-Saxon tradition in ways which even the "inferior races" from eastern and southern Europe could accept. The major thrust of all of these programs was to protect the morality and the institutions of the new world from the danger-laden onslaught of the old.

One of the educator's great fears was that the moral fiber of the nation was coming apart. Particularly under immigrant influence, politics was being corrupted, promiscuity was increasing, and the drinking of alcoholic beverages was becoming a scourge. Thus, Jane Robbins, a teacher from Pennsylvania, set up classes in the coal fields to combat what she perceived to be the immorality of the immigrant worker. Her classes reinforced time-honored moral maxims and were, in the process, "of great value in preventing the formation of the drinking habit."[44] Other teachers saw in sex hygiene classes a means of preserving conventional morality. One teacher wrote that such programs were the best means "of so directing the association of the sexes as to suppress familiarity and to develop becoming modesty." This teacher, like most in her profession, believed herself bequeathed of the task of perserving American moral and cultural values through

---

[43] *Ibid.*, pp. 26-27.

[44] U.S., Bureau of Education, *Education of the Immigrant*, 1913, Bulletin No. 51, p. 17.

her own personal example. She continued, rather ecstatically:

> [The teacher should] serve as a radiation center for immeasurable suggestion for the boys and girls entrusted to her care. Under the spell of her hypnotic power, youth and maiden may take on purity of life, nobleness of purpose, devotedness to ideals and beauty of character. . . . Happy that pupil who has one of this company for his teacher, provided that teacher lives always on the Olympic heights of character, surrounded by the eternal snows of purity, and reflecting ever the unfading sunlight of intelligence and of righteousness.[45]

Another educator concurred that sex hygiene classes were necessary to combat the "social evil" which was growing at an alarming rate. In similar phraseology he asserted the need of this training because "of the influence of chastity, strength of character and body, and the profound influence of noble manhood and womanhood upon the future welfare of the race."[46] As the threat to the American race intensified in the minds of the educators, they lashed out for ever widening conformity to ever more ambiguous principles. If only the wretched of the slums could be made noble, righteous and chaste, then Mulberry Street could become the Olympic heights, and the American race could yet be saved! The educators had set for themselves a Herculean project indeed.

And ambitiously did they pursue it. In every city with a sizeable immigrant community, the educators established night schools for foreigners, segregated immigrants for special courses in day classes, recruited bilingual teachers, and conducted scrubbings for those foreign pupils whom they found particularly offensive. In addition, the immigrants' presence stimulated redoubled efforts for manual training programs, co-op schools, domestic service training, home economic courses, and compulsory public education. Educators had launched a major effort in the movement of Americanize the immigrant.[47]

---

[45] H. F. M. Gregg, "Social Hygiene," *Education*, XXXIII (October, 1912), p. 104.

[46] Harold Molter, "Practical Suggestions for the Teaching of Sex Hygiene," *Education*, XXXIV (October, 1913), p. 97.

[47] For general accounts of the efforts of the educators on behalf of immigrants, see Cremin, *Transformation of the Schools*, John Higham, *Strangers in the Land* (New Brunswick, N.J.: Rutgers University, 1967), and Edward George Hartmann, *The Movement to Americanize the Immigrant* (New York: Columbia University Press, 1948).

In almost all of the major cities, the schools established special classes for immigrants. Common ingredients to most of these classes were heavy doses of patriotism, purity, and paternalism. Joseph Wade, district superintendent of schools for New York City, explained that the immigrant had to be segregated because of his need for guidance in English and good citizenship. He even suggested that Jewish students be segregated from Italians because Jews were "more ambitious."[48] One of the primary reasons for segregated classes was the presumed inferiority of non-Anglo-Saxon stock. M. Catherine Mahy, a high school English teacher in Providence, complained that the "foreign element" in her special classes were not, "heirs of the priceless heredity of English culture" and that they were badly in need of, "good American citizenship." Among the books she selected for her foreigners were:

> Andrew's, *The Perfect Tribute*, Hale's, *A Man Without A Country*, Lincoln's Speeches, Webster's Bunker Hill Oration, Mr. Boardman's excellent collection of American speeches and such other selections . . . as may appeal to the impassioned Jewish or Italian nature.

Yet lest she be misunderstood, Mahy assured her readers that under no circumstances did she "advocate leveling our entire English course to the plane of the foreigner thus depriving our American youth of their rich inheritance."[49]

The same aura of condescension and the demand for moral and political orthodoxy permeated the night schools established for the immigrant's benefit. Concerned about the "poorer quality of immigrants," Mary Knox, principal of Manhattan School No. 15, asserted that immigrants should be forced to attend night school. There they would learn, "the duties of citizenship and how to guard against the dangers of a great city . . . [such as] truancy, games of chance on the street, throwing dice, haunts of vice, candy stores where cigarettes are sold and gambling outfits installed, and moving picture shows where coarse scenes are exhibited."[50] All of the immigrant night schools offered instruction in English and citizenship.

---

[48] U.S. Bureau of Education, *Education of the Immigrant*, p. 24.

[49] M. Catherine Mahy, "The Differentiation of Teaching English Classes in the High School," *Education*, XXXVI (May, 1916), pp. 577-80.

[50] U.S. Bureau of Education, *Education of Immigrants*, pp. 29-30.

Yet neither the fear of moral decline nor the demand for political and cultural conformity completely explain why the educational community so wholeheartedly supported the exploitive co-op industrial training movement. However, both these motivations provide important insights into the pedagogic mind. Certainly the educators could have been more critical of the industrial co-op experiment. Clearly alternatives were open to them. The educators could have pressured local industry for more equitable wages for its apprentices and co-op students. They could have been more solicitous of the advice of skilled and unskilled labor. They could have shortened the duration of the training courses so that young men would qualify for skilled level wages in one year instead of four. In short, they could have made their influence pronounced in the education industrial partnership.

Unluckily for the immigrant, the educators did none of these things. They were uncritical partners because they shared the corporate community's view of the world. The United States was entering an era of industrial and technocratic revolution. To meet the demands of the new era, the nation must supply industry with the necessary number of workers possessing the necessary skills. To the educator, the line between industrial needs and national needs became indistinct. Loyalty to America and loyalty to its corporate structure became one and the same. Teachers believed that the preservation of the "American race" was predicated on the survival of American capitalism. Thus the school teacher who believed his task to be the protection of the American cultural heritage thought also that he must protect and promote the American industrial state. With reasoning such as this, Charles Wheelock, assistant commissioner of education for the state of New York, announced with a clear conscience that, "the New York high school stands ready to ally itself with the dominant interests of any town and to give vocational instruction demanded by such interests. . . ."[51]

Since a capitalist and a patriot were one, the educator concurred with the industrialist that there was no better crucible in which to mold immigrants into Americans than the factory. S. J. Vaughan, head of the department of manual arts in an Illinois high school, described the moral qualities which his program could best instill. They were "honesty, purpose, ambition, discretion, sobriety and punctuality." He asserted that the industrial world was best suited to impart these qualities. "When in the school printshop," he boasted:

> The boys nudge each other and whisper, "Gee!
> This is just the way they do it downtown."
> It is this idealized view of the industrial
> world which I seek to take advantage of . . .

---

[51] New York State, Department of Education, *Ninth Annual Report*, 1913, p. 128.

in laying the foundation for future citizenship.
This is the first phase. . . . [This naivete]
provides a splendid basis for the philosophy of
both life and of industry.⁵²

Perhaps the most interesting example of the educator's frightened quest for conformity was provided by the editor of an education journal. Stressing the necessity of national loyalty and a unity of purpose, Charles H. Johnston quoted the following passage from the fascist philosopher--General Friedrich Bernhardi:

Only an army of warlike and patriotic people can
achieve anything really great. After the school
. . . [which will] furnish all with patriotic
sentiments . . . then the government must control a strong and aggressive national press.

Interestingly, Johnston quoted Bernhardi not in criticism but in praise and envy. He lamented that a national call for militant patriotism would be ineffective in the United States because of the diversity of ethnic backgrounds. Germans rallied behind their common traditions of national pride and military prowess. The United States, on the other hand, was divided and weakened by its many races with their lack of a common loyalty. Johnston's prescription was both vague and frightening. The United States "must establish on a national basis some moral equivalent for the so effective nationalistic, martially patriotic bases underlying some of the European systems." Another educator, Edwin S. Todd of Miami (Ohio) University, maintained that the welfare of the nation was seriously jeopardized by traditional attachment to individual rights. He recommended that such cornerstones of individualism as the Bill of Rights, Declaration of Independence, and the Preamble, be deemphasized. In their place, the new emphasis, especially to the young, must be on the good and security of the state. "It is of supreme importance," Todd pleaded:

That the young citizen be made to understand
the philosophy underlying the transition from
the old individualistic declaration that the
welfare of the individual was impaired as soon
as the State curtailed his civic rights, to
the new philosophy which declares a seeming
paradox, namely, that the welfare of the individual in the industrial world is bound up
in the welfare of the state.⁵³

---

⁵²S. J. Vaughan, "The Moral Significance of the Vocational Motive," *Education*, XXXIII (June, 1913), pp. 593-97.

⁵³Charles H. Johnston, "The Nation as a Participant in Public

For Johnston, Todd, and many other educators who feared the hordes of barbarians infiltrating through Ellis Island, something drastic had to be done. Teachers must use their classrooms, their shop benches, and their local industries, if necessary, to superimpose upon the invader that "moral equivalent" which might yet convert him.

In the final analysis, educators refused to see the seamy side of the co-op schools because they were desperately pre-occupied. All that America represented, and all the homilies, clichés, and eternal verities in which they trusted were under seige. Educators saw themselves fighting on the cultural ramparts of their nation. Education had to be bent to meet the needs of a nation struggling for survival. If education imparted the harsh discipline of a co-op school or even the martial spirit of a Prussian training program, so much the better. In order to save democracy, many educators seemed willing to destroy it.

Captain Douglas MacArthur, in 1909, pressed home this theme before the Commission on National Aid to Vocational Education. To the future General of the Army, the most important function of the army in peace time was to train Americans in the profession of arms and to turn them back into society properly militarized. He declared that the United States Army:

> Is the greatest educational institution in the government. . . . The real intent now, of the army is to make the army . . . a school clearinghouse to teach the profession of arms, to make the enlistment a short one, the training intensive, and to pass the man back into civil life in the shortest possible time with such military training. . . .[54]

More disturbing than MacArthur's vision of a citizenship trained by the army as quasi-professional military, was the commission's reaction to his testimony. MacArthur provoked not a ripple of dissent, not a single request for clarification, not even a hostile question from the commission of educators and congressmen. To the commission, MacArthur's was a viable alternative in the quest for national unity.

The educators represented a volatile admixture of a number of attitudes. They feared the pitfalls of cultural pluralism, they longed for a foolproof system to Americanize foreigners, they felt their cultural heritage slipping away, retreating under seige.

Education," *Education Administration and Supervision*, I (February, 1915), pp. 154-56. Edwin S. Todd, "An Economic Basis for Civics Teaching," *Education*, XXXII (March, 1912), p. 442.

[54]*Vocational Aid Commission Report*, p. 122.

Because of these phobias, teachers were willing to consign the ethnic minorities to an admittedly inferior education. If permitted into the academic classroom, the immigrant could not be allowed to lower the educational standards of Anglo-Saxon stock and so had to be segregated and given special readings. If admitted to vocational training, the immigrant was to accept large does of harsh discipline and lessons in national and industrial loyalty. Nor was it as though the educators did not realize the second-rate education to which they hoped to assign the less fit. The superintendent of schools for the state of Pennsylvania shrewdly observed that:

> The loudest advocates of the trade school act as if they considered that kind of an education a good thing for their neighbor's son, but for their own son, they invariably prefer . . . a different type of education.[55]

If the industrial training movement did more harm than good, it was because it served too many masters. It supplied cheap labor, becalmed those who saw themselves as defenders of the faith, and introduced foreigners to their proper place in American society. Perhaps industrial educationists could have been more successful had they only taken more to heart the needs of those newly arrived whom they purported to help.

---

[55]State of Pennsylvania, *Report of the Superintendent of Public Instruction,* 1912, p. 7.

CHAPTER IV

THE YMCA AND THE POLITICS OF CO-OPTATION

> "[YMCA] work produces splendid results on the economic side. . . . All intelligent railroad officials are learning that this work is a great thing for the investor."[1]
>
> John J. McCook
> YMCA Executive

> "The result of our small investment in the YMCA is almost beyond our belief. Men who formerly got drunk are sober. Whereas we had trouble getting men, there is [now] a waiting list. No local strikes now, but the best of good will."[2]
>
> West Virginia Coal Operator

> "The YMCA does not attempt to adjust issues [between management and labor] but it creates a spirit which enlarges the field of agreement. It is not partisan. It is more than neutral: it is mutual."[3]
>
> YMCA "Zone of Agreement" Policy

---

[1] John J. McCook, "The Work of the YMCA Among Railroad Men," *The Jubilee of Work for Young Men in North America*, ed. by Jubilee Convention of North American YMCA's (New York: International Committee of YMCA's, 1901), p. 145.

[2] "Reports of the Industrial Committee of the Young Men's Christian Association," YMCA Historical Library, New York City, November, 1915.

[3] Galen Fisher, *Public Affairs and the YMCA* (New York: Association Press, 1948), p. 72.

> "The gentleman who provides the fund from which the class [a trade class for children under legal working age held at the YMCA] is sustained is the employer of these boys; it would offend him deeply for us to discontinue the class."[4]
>
> YMCA Local Secretary

Unlike the educators, settlement workers, and charity volunteers, the Young Men's Christian Association enlisted in the cultural cold war almost by inadvertence. The YMCA transplanted its peculiar brand of urban evangelism from London to Boston in 1851. Almost immediately, the "Y's" religious fervor brought it into mission and welfare work. The YMCA thus became involved in the plight of the urban worker, particularly during depressions or periods of seasonal unemployment. As the railroads flung the labor force far and wide during the post Civil War period, the YMCA joined other religious groups in competition for its redemption. But YMCA organizers soon discovered that they could not convert the worker until they had converted his employer. The "Y" needed facilities (often only a reading room to start) and funds, both of which only management could supply. The YMCA railroad program, expanding enormously between 1870 and the turn of the century, brought the "Y" into contact with the railroad worker primarily because of business' donations of money, land, and sometimes buildings. In the words of the "Association's" most noted authority, the railroad program, "was a mission to the aristocracy rather than the rank and file of labor." It "was the movement's one markedly effective approach to the working class in the nineteenth century."[5]

Using the "from-the-top" approach of the railroad program as a precedent, the YMCA developed its immigration programs during the early years of the twentieth century. Among institutions offering programs for immigrants, none were as comprehensive as those developed by the Association. The YMCA placed its agents at the European ports, on board the vessels, and at American ports such as Ellis Island. In the cities, where the immigrants settled, the "Y" offered employment service, room and board at reasonable rates, Christian guidance, and

---

[4] Ernest H. Abbott, "The Exodus from Philistia," *The Outlook*, LXXXI (December 30, 1905), pp. 1073-1077.

[5] C. Howard Hopkins, *The History of the YMCA in North America* (New York: Association Press, 1951), p. 277. Hopkins' work is by far the most comprehensive of all historical studies of the YMCA. However, it is largely narrative rather than analytical and contains only scant information on the immigration programs. For an extensive discussion of the "Y's" early development and its railroad program, see Chapters 1, 2, and 5.

courses in English, civics, history, and hygiene. Once the immigrant found a job, he was likely to encounter YMCA classes during his lunch hour. Even after work, the immigrant might find YMCA workers teaching him at the neighborhood night school. But from the European port to the night school, the YMCA could not escape the influence of its benefactors. The "mission to the aristocracy" was unable to develop a program entirely in the interest of the peasantry.

A program so extensive as the YMCA's did not come about without considerable pressure or without opposition. The pressures were threefold. First, the "Y," like all other urban institutions of the early twentieth century, found its neighborhoods inundated with "new" immigrants badly in need of help. Second, one faction of YMCA leadership began to move away from the narrow religious definition of the "Y's" purpose, and insisted that the Association involve itself in social betterment. Finally, business interests, on whom the YMCA was financially dependent, began to see the "Y" as a valuable instrument in the process of making immigrant labor reliable, efficient and nonradical. But the opposition to the immigration program had to be overcome. It too came from three sources. First, from within the YMCA hierarchy, the old guard resisted and opposed measures advocated by the activists. Second, the immigrants themselves showed occasional resentment and hostility toward YMCA efforts on their behalf. Third, a few business leaders resisted the idea of spending company funds for programs not essential to the welfare of their companies.

To understand the relationship between the YMCA and local business, one must keep in mind that in this era before United Fund and Community Chest the YMCA was necessarily dependent upon the local business community for financial backing. Thus, the "Y" was under constant pressure to provide services and programs useful and inoffensive to its benefactors.

Whatever problems this paternalism imposed, the "Y's" relationship with business paid enormous dividends. Between 1900 and 1916, two hundred and ninety buildings were constructed comprising an aggregate annual cost exceeding seven million dollars on two occasions. This period has correctly been characterized as "the greatest building period in American Association history."[6] Due largely to the expansion of its railroad program, the YMCA was a multimillion dollar corporation by 1900. During 1901 alone the YMCA erected seven million dollars worth of new buildings in twenty-three cities and substantial additions to buildings in fifteen other cities. Fifteen additional railroad buildings were opened. Total real estate carried an estimated value of 23 million dollars, 400 buildings, 1500 associations and 325,000 members. Five years later, in 1906, the number of members had grown to over 405,000, the number of associations to 1868, buildings to 552 and real estate value was set at 34.6 million

---

[6]Ibid., p. 456.

dollars.[7] Business often proved reliable in case of emergency also. For example, when the New York "Y" had accumulated a $300,000 debt, William E. and Cleveland H. Dodge contributed $50,000 apiece while John D. Rockefeller and J. P. Morgan gave $100,000 each. The "Y" was one hundred percent dependent upon contributions, almost all of which came from business sources.[8]

One interesting example of the excellent response of the business community, was the rebuilding of the YMCA in San Francisco after the old one was destroyed by fire in 1906. In two months, not only did the "Y" raise the $500,000 needed, but it also raised enough to pay the Association's general secretary's travel expenses and four months salary as well.[9]

The sales pitch employed by the YMCA was indeed persuasive. In approaching railroad executives, steel corporation officials, or textile mill operators, the YMCA representative argued along three lines. First, if the company would build a YMCA or at least offer some space for its use (a foot in the door!), the working men would have available good, clean recreational facilities and Christian influence. This was not likely to convince the owner that he should construct a building, pay the secretary (executive-manager of each YMCA Association) and supply land. The representative then pointed out that without YMCA facilities, workers frequented saloons, reported for work inebriated, and performed inefficiently on the job. The "Y" was a morale booster and men with good morale worked harder, more efficiently and with less complaint. One YMCA executive enthusiastically demonstrated in dollars and cents the worth of the YMCA

---

[7]"A Great Instrument," *The Outlook*, LXXII (September 6, 1902), p. 14. "Young Men's Christian Association Annual Dinner," *The Outlook*, LXXXIV (November 17, 1917), p. 648.

[8]Terry Donoghue, *An Event on Mercer Street* (place not given: by the author, n.d.), p. 61. This volume may be found at the Olin Graduate Library, Cornell University, Ithaca, New York. Financial Report, January 15, 1910, "Reports of the Industrial Committee of the Young Men's Christian Association," YMCA Historical Library, New York City. These reports were of immeasurable use to this study and will be hereafter cited as "Industrial Committee Reports." Pagination of these reports is irregular but will be given when possible.

[9]Clifford M. Drury, *San Francisco YMCA: One Hundred Years by the Golden Gate 1853-1953* (Glendale, California: Arthur H. Clarke Company, 1963), pp. 128-29. The author supplies a complete list of contributors. An interesting account and listing of business benefactors of the railroad associations is provided in Richard C. Morse, *My Life With Young Men* (New York: Association Press, 1918), p. 399. See also Ward Adair, *Memories of George Warburton* (New York: J. J. Little and Ives and Company, n.d.), p. 23.

to the companies which employed its services. He claimed that the "Y" contributed to the development of a "happy home" by creating the proper cultural and moral environment. This beneficial influence promoted workers who arrived on the job with a clear mind, pure heart, and high morale. How much more efficient must such a worker be, he asked rhetorically, than "the man who goes to his work from the saloon or some other low resort?"

Even more crucial than the YMCA's moral influence, the executive maintained, was its direct economic benefit to the participating industries and railroads. He continued:

> This work produces splendid results on the economic as well as on the moral side. All intelligent railroad officials are learning that this work is a great thing for the investor. When the holders of the securities of our railroads fully understand what it means to have these association houses at their division points, they will demand their establishment. I am convinced that in the future investors will not have as much confidence in a railroad manager who has not the sense and intelligence to see the advantage of such work, and they will prefer to have someone else manage the railroads in which they are interested.

One railroad executive concurred, referring to the YMCA as the "greatest agency for railroad morale that has ever been discovered." Another added:

> When you talk about the care of our men away from home, you are talking a language we can understand. We cannot escape responsibility for that and it is no trouble to justify the appropriation of railroad funds when they are expended to make our men more fit for duty.[10]

Evidently, the YMCA was not greeted with open arms by the local saloon keepers. At Cripple Creek, Colorado, where the "Y" had convinced the gold mine operators to build a $25,000 YMCA, the saloon owners vowed to donate "$500 for a wide open town." C. C. Michener, industrial secretary of the "Y," reported to his superiors, "I have not time to describe the conditions in that wicked place [Cripple Creek]." To those who wanted to keep the west wild, Michener was

---

[10] John J. McCook, "The Work of the YMCA Among Railroad Men," *The Jubillee of Work for Young Men in North America*, ed. by Jubilee Convention of North American YMCA's (New York: International Committee of YMCA's, 1901), p. 145. Adair, *George Warburton*, p. 26.

about as welcome as Carrie Nation.[11]

Another persuasive ingredient of the YMCA sales pitch was its antiradicalism. The Association correctly pictured itself as a valuable asset in fighting the influence of socialism and the International Workers of the World and in calming strike situations. The Industrial Committee collected and apparently used statements from happy industrialists who benefited from the YMCA's beneficent influence. For example, the president of a Virginia coal mine wrote "If that YMCA Secretary had been here, our strike in which blood was shed, never would have occurred." The vice-president of a copper mining company added, "It is gratifying to the officers of our company to note the active and useful services of the Association during the recent strike." Still a third, a coal operator from West Virginia attested, "The result of our small investment in the YMCA is almost beyond our belief. Men who formerly got drunk are sober. Whereas we had trouble getting men, there is [now] a waiting list. No local strikes now, but the best of good will." The "Y" had won such a reputation as a labor tranquilizer that in November, 1915, the Tennessee Coal and Iron Company brought together representatives of three troubled industrial communities in order to "cooperate with other industries in establishing Associations."[12] In short, to many business leaders, the YMCA represented a way to insure labor peace without having to confront issues such as wages, hours and safety measures.

This is not to suggest that the YMCA's industrial representatives were insincere in their appeals to industrial executives.

---

[11]"Industrial Committee Reports," May 1907 and September 1906. The following excerpt from the reports gives an excellent account of YMCA activities. "The following are some of the places where work has been started: At Burnham, Pa., the location of the Standard Steel Works, a branch of the Baldwin Locomotive Works; at Ishpeming, Mich., by the Oliver Manufacturing Company, and the Cleveland Cliffs Iron Company; at Calumet, Mich., by the Calumet & Hecla Company; at Wilmerding, Pa., by the Westinghouse Air Brake Company; at Lincoln, N.H., by the Henry Brothers Lumber Company; at Tacoma, Wash., by the Tacoma Smelter Company, a branch of the American Smelting and Refining Company. There have been two buildings provided for in the bituminous coal region of Pennsylvania. There have also been two buildings provided for in the Ohio coal fields. Five companies have united in the promotion of a building at Carteret, N.J. A gold mining company and a silver mining company at Telluride, Colo., have each assisted in the erection of a building. The Cooper Queen Company and the Calumet & Arizona Copper Company, at Bisbee, Ariz., and the Tacoma & St. Paul Lumber Company, at Tacoma, Wash., have also organized associations. In addition to these, there are at least a dozen more places where work is already started."

[12]Ibid., February, 1915, November, 1914, and November, 1915.

Indeed, most YMCA leaders saw themselves as the vanguard of opposition to labor radicalism. Musing about the difficulty of the fight against radicals, C. C. Michener wrote:

> If the great body of the working men of our country are to be helped, we must expect large things from the city associations. It is largely in these cities that the evil social influences are at work and where extreme socialistic agitation is most actively carried on. The working men of the cities, therefore, become more of a menace and need to be more carefully looked after.[13]

In the same report, Michener criticized "these socialists delivering their attacks upon the nation and its leading men." He explained that "these speakers are usually working men. The working men's communities are being flooded with tons of printed matter, attacking the fundamental principles of the Republic." Michener saw the YMCA as a "corrective to these socialistic influences."[14]

By the early twentieth century then, the YMCA had established its approach to industry. It promised employers that an investment in the YMCA would pay dividends in sober, efficient, uncomplaining and non-radical workers. The same argument would soon be used to set up a whole series of programs to Americanize, sanitize, and promote efficiency among the hordes of new immigrant workers. Business proved overwhelmingly responsive to these overtures. In a magazine article in late 1906, Michener looked back over the preceding year's progress. He proudly announced that business had contributed about $400,000 in YMCA club houses alone which he called "a successful competitor with the saloon." During 1906, Michener summarized, the YMCA constructed or began construction of YMCA buildings in partnership with over twenty-four companies in nearly as many states.[15]

The usual procedure for Michener or one of his field representatives was to visit a company, make a study of its labor problem, outline the programs and facilities needed, then appoint a secretary when the company agreed to pay him an acceptable salary and to present

---

[13] *Ibid.*, "Report of C. C. Michener," p. 3. This report was read at the fall meeting of the Industrial Committee, Atlantic City, New Jersey, September, 1906.

[14] *Ibid.*, p. 6.

[15] C. C. Michener, "Industrial YMCA's Work," *Textile Manufacturer's Journal* (December 29, 1906), p. 97. This article was found in the "Industrial Committee Reports," 1907.

the YMCA with the facilities. Westinghouse Airbrake Company, for example, contributed $110,000 to erect a YMCA facility for its employees, while Judge Elbert H. Gary personally donated a $100,000 building for one of his U.S. Steel plants, two years later. The Gary gift was supplemented by "four lots" of land. Jones and Laughlin soon followed with a $50,000 building and a promise of $5,000 annually for maintenance. A brief excerpt from Michener's Industrial Committee report for 1905, reveals much about the YMCA operations.

> I have investigated this year seventeen different industrial communities and have made written reports on ten of these. The Westinghouse Air Brake Company has before it a plan for a building which will cost about $100,000. The decision on this will come at the September meeting. Nothing of course must be said publicly regarding this until something definite is passed. There are two manufacturing cities in Massachusetts where companies have decided to erect buildings during this next year. The names of the places and the companies cannot yet be made public. The United States Steel Corporation have within the past few weeks given $2,000 towards the indebtedness of the association at their works at Lorain, Ohio, in addition to the $1200 which they have been giving annually. They have increased their annual appropriation, beginning with September 1st, to $2500 a year. They also have before them a plan to double the capacity of their present building. A decision on this will be reached in a short time. Several other very important concerns have been investigating the association since the reports have been submitted and at fall meetings of their boards of directors there will be decisions reached by these corporations. Immediately following this conference I shall go for two weeks to Colorado to investigate two of the largest gold mining communities, viz: Telluride and Cripple Creek. I shall also have several trips in connection with the companies already dealt with. A few new concerns are still waiting for investigation.[16]

---

[16]"Industrial Committee Reports," September, 1905, September, 1906, December, 1906, May, 1907, and June, 1909.

At times, the YMCA could be a rather tough negotiator. It refused to establish an association at the Tacoma Smelting Company in 1906 because the plant manager could secure only one-half the amount needed. Only after the manager agreed to find the rest of the money did the Industrial Committee agree to organize in Tacoma. That same year, the Pennsylvania YMCA Anthracite and Bituminous Department Committee made it a policy to refuse to establish any more associations on a voluntary basis. It resolved that "no new associations be organized among employees except where adequate buildings can be secured and a general secretary employed." The policy evidently paid off handsomely because a further report boasted that "Corporations are willing to give larger salaries than have been given by railway companies. . . ."[17]

All of this prosperity was not without its attendant misgivings within the YMCA power structure. The YMCA faced a three pronged dilemma. On the one hand, if it chose to preserve and emphasize its Christian-religious orientation, it could not provide the services to entice the financial support of those many industries which needed a labor tranquilizer and anti-radical agent. Yet if the YMCA moved into social activism and thus identified itself with reform, it might lose business support anyway. Finally, if the YMCA became identified too closely with industrial interests, it might lose the trust of the very workingmen which its programs were designed to attract. In short, business sponsorship brought with it a host of problems.

One influential group of YMCA purists desired to keep the YMCA solely a religious organization and particularly wanted to avoid involvement in social and political issues. Some, described by a critic as "men of reactionary mind, of fantastic theology and of separatist tendencies," went so far as to oppose the introduction of games of any kind into the Railroad Association rooms asserting that YMCA facilities must be used for religious purposes only.[18] But most of the purists had other objections to activism. Led by Loring W. Messer, Robert R. McBurney, and George Warburton, association secretaries of Chicago, Cleveland and New York respectively, the old guard insisted that social involvement would spell disaster. These leaders agreed with Messer who wrote that the drift toward social involvement represented "prevention rather than rescue, construction rather than reconstruction, formation rather than reformation."[19]

---

[17]"Report of C. C. Michener," pp. 2, 4, 5.

[18]Adair, *George Warburton*, p. 42.

[19]Emmett Dedmon, *Great Enterprises* (New York: Rand McNally, 1957), pp. 210-211.

These attitudes distilled into an iron-clad principle for the conservatives--avoid political involvement. McBurney had set down some guidelines in the late 1880's from which he expected the YMCA not to deviate. One of its most important principles was "when questions of moral reform become political party questions our association as such, can have no connection with them."[20] Perhaps more central to the objections against activism, however, was a deeply rooted conservatism and an antipathy toward the plight of the disadvantaged. These men saw the United States as the land of milk and honey and the reformers as simply misguided, bleeding hearts. McBurney replied to a friend in January 1897, concerning the campaign of William Jennings Bryan. He expressed relief that the nation had not gone for Bryan in 1896 because even though business had not improved much, it would have been even worse had Bryan been elected. He answered some arguments his friend had evidently made on Bryan's behalf. As for Bryan's being the champion of the downtrodden, he noted that all Americans during these years of depression were suffering. But, McBurney queried, "What profit would there be in doing anything else than patiently bearing the times through which we are passing?" If conditions were bad and their causes obscure, it would do no good to agitate and rabble rouse. After all, he asserted, "we are a free people and I really do not know that anybody is downtrodden in this land." McBurney's colleague had complained of the crushing weight of the eastern banking concerns (whom he referred to as "Shylocks") upon the already overburdened farmer of the heartland. In his dismissal of his friend's arguments McBurney revealed his deeply-rooted traditionalism and conservatism. "You speak of Shylocks," he countered:

> I suppose there are some; but are not the people of the West to blame for incurring such financial obligations with their eyes open? Why do they place themselves in the hands of the Shylocks? Is not their difficulty largely due to their overhaste to get rich? . . . I do not consider such people downtrodden at all. I would say that they were unwise. As to the price of farm produce, I do not see how that could be altered. We cannot force up the price of wheat; if there is overcultivation, of course, prices would be low. Notwithstanding all the drawbacks in our land, it is the Eden of the earth for men in all conditions of life.[21]

---

[20] L. L. Doggett, *The Life of Robert R. McBurney* (Cleveland, Ohio: F. M. Barton Company, 1902), p. 145.

[21] *Ibid.*, pp. 151-52.

Some in the YMCA governing structure asserted that the Association was already quite political because it was closely identified with its business benefactors. This business paternalism presented the twin dangers of undermining the ideals and goals of the YMCA and of alienating the working people the YMCA was supposed to help. As head of the Industrial Committee, C. C. Michener sensed the mistrust and suspicion of the working men, but he was inclined to blame them on the lack of sanity of the union leadership. In 1903 Michener reported that working with union men (primarily foreign) was much more difficult than working with the more Americanized railroad brothers. He complained that the "whole attitude of working men is one of suspicion." He found it puzzling that union leaders were much more recalcitrant than railroad brotherhood leaders had been. He suspected that this was due to the "ignorance and prejudice" of the rank and file who were therefore easily manipulated by their demagogic leaders. He warned that as long as the union leadership remained powerful, "there will always be trouble--association or no association." Labor unions were therefore, *ipso facto* a threat to the relationship between the YMCA and industry. New approaches were necessary, Michener argued, in order to circumvent and neutralize the union organizers. He predicted that although the close cooperation of the railroad brotherhoods no longer could be expected, appearances had to be maintained. "Work [to establish YMCA programs] must begin," he concluded, "so far as the men know, with themselves." Needless to say, Michener thought it best not to inform the workers that the YMCA was working closely with management in order to undermine the power of their union leaders.[22] Michener clearly wished to conceal from the workers the YMCA's intimate relationship with management. But he may have allowed hindsight to obscure the difficulties of earlier days in railroad organization, for one historian of the movement has written of the railroad workers for the New York Central, "The men looked askance at the proposal [to build a YMCA] fearing some infringement on their rights or some ulterior motive on the part of the company."[23]

Others in the YMCA realized that the suspicion of the workers was symptomatic of a larger problem. The YMCA had developed a business mentality and its goals and programs had been seriously compromised. One authority on Association affairs writing in 1946, saw the issue clearly:

> It is sometimes assumed that frequent intervention
> by those who are relatively powerful financially
> constitutes a large factor in the policies and

---

[22]"Industrial Committee Reports," September, 1903.

[23]Frank W. Ober, *James Stokes, Pioneer* (New York: Association Press, 1921), p. 49.

management of organizations such as the Young
Men's Christian Association. This control, it is
assumed, is accomplished both through formal representation in boards, through substantial contributions toward operating costs, and sometimes
through systems of auditing and fiscal control.
So long as programs are devised that seem to
require facilities and expenditures greater than
the constituency served can be expected to pay for
fully, it is inevitable that such representatives
of powerful economic sources should have a part in
at least decisions relating to expenditure. . . .
Where strong industrial corporations sponsor and
contribute to Association work among their own
employees, sometimes in buildings erected for
this purpose on their company property, a somewhat more complex type of control results. Such
programs are, from the standpoint of the companies
involved, a part of their own "welfare" programs.
. . . But it should not be assumed that, inevitably and in all instances, the exercise of
such control was designing and sinister. It was,
and is, often a reflection of the deepest good
will and concern by the industrial management.
For the YMCA serving in such circumstances the
issue is undoubtedly whether it shall long continue
to work as an integral part of a paternalistic
regime. It might elect, rather, to stake the continuance of its contacts and services among
such workers upon the interest, contributions,
and control of the workers served. If, as
seems undoubtedly to have been the case, the
paternalistic system in industry was closely
related, generally speaking, to a low wage scale,
it would appear that the marked advance of the
general wage rates offers, for really the first
time, a valid occasion for complete review and
perhaps reorganization of policy.[24]

Another Association historian has observed that because of the "unconscious bias" of the Association secretaries toward their business benefactors, the YMCA "was doubtless looked upon by both management and labor as a sop to labor to retard unionization."[25]

---

[24] Owen Pence, *The YMCA and Social Need: A Study of Institutional Adaptation* (New York: Association Press, 1946), pp. 325-29.

[25] Galen Fisher, *Public Affairs and the YMCA* (New York: Association Press, 1948), pp. 90-93.

An even greater danger presented by business paternalism was the gradual erosion of the YMCA's purpose, the compromising of its goals, and the subservience of its priorities to business needs. In theory this did not occur because the Industrial Committee followed a "Zone of Agreement" policy. This policy stated that the YMCA "does not attempt to adjust issues [between management and labor] but it creates a spirit which enlarges the field of agreement. It is not partisan. It is more than neutral: it is mutual."[26] But in practice, the YMCA was partisan, it was neither mutual nor neutral. When local business asked for classes or seminars which it needed, the YMCA was at its service. The Association offered seminars in everything from public utility economics to plumbing instruction for child laborers. In one case the "Y" established a trade class for children under legal working age. When questioned, the local secretary replied that he could not halt the class because "the gentleman who provides the fund from which the class is sustained is the employer of these boys; it would offend him deeply for us to discontinue the class."[27] On the eve of the immigration programs, one observer noted that the YMCA was colored by commercialism and dominated by wealthy business leaders. He perceived that:

> Under such leaders the Association has been endowed with commercial temperment. Its standards of success are . . . [those] valid in commercial circles; its ethical point of view, that of the tradesmen; its understanding of its duties to society, that of the ordinary capitalist; its religion, that of a practical man of affairs.

Thus, the YMCA, like business, measured success in numbers: how many new buildings erected, how much land donated, how many bodies in occupancy, how many pamphlets distributed. The same critic summarized well the YMCA's malaise when he remarked: "The social ethics of the Association is, by inheritance, the social ethics of the business world. . . . Its religion has been a masculine, efficient, business religion."[28]

---

[26]*Ibid.*, p. 72.

[27]Abbott, "The Exodus from Philistia," pp. 1073-77.

[28]*Ibid.* For an example of the kind of seminars offered by the YMCA for business, see George W. Wharton, "Business Men at School," *The Outlook*, LXXXVII (October 12, 1907), pp. 303-06. Also an entire public utility seminar is recorded in New York West Side YMCA, *Public Utility Economics* (New York: The Finance Forum, 1915).

Even in the face of strong local antagonism the YMCA's allegience to business often did not sway. In one midwestern city, for example, the Association could get no press coverage for its campaign to build a YMCA. The people were apathetic and lower level leaders in the city accused the "Y" boosters, local business executives, of being corrupt. Evidently, the financial leaders whom the Association chose as partners had recently raised $400,000 in public subscriptions to promote a new industry which failed. The Association secretary involved staunchly defended his business benefactors. "The 'crooks, and demagogues' on the committees," he contended, "were guilty of being good businessmen, good lodge members, and regular church attendants. . . ."[29]

Such then was the nature of the relationship between business and the YMCA as the Association turned its attention to the problems of immigrants. Business leaders saw the immigrants not so much as people, but as inefficient workers inclined to be safety hazards; not as citizens, but as potential radicals and labor agitators. Such an assessment deeply influenced the Association's immigration programs. This is not to suggest that there were no YMCA workers deeply committed to the human needs of immigrants, but rather that those so committed worked within a structure and a system which tended to compromise their efforts. Thus, when Dr. Peter Roberts began his work as head of the Immigration Division of the Industrial Committee in 1907, he had at once to serve two masters, immigrant workers and their employers-- a compromise those who took the option of social activism were forced to make.

Despite the growing problems presented by the arrival of large numbers of immigrants upon the urban-industrial scene, the YMCA was relatively late in starting its own program for immigrants. Not until February, 1907, did the Industrial Committee officially turn its attention to the plight of the immigrant in America. On the 16th of that month, the YMCA convened a "conference of denominational representation" in Philadelphia to discuss the subject "How the Industrial Department of the International Committee of the Young Men's Christian Association May Become of Greater Service in Dealing With the Problems Which Arise Out of the Presence in This Country of Large Numbers of People of Alien Races."[30] After long discussion, the conferees resolved to establish a comprehensive immigration program designed to assist the immigrant at the embarkation and debarkation ports, on

---

[29]"An Adventure in Public Opinion," *The Outlook*, CII (September 7, 1912), p. 42. The name of the city was not given.

[30]"Report of the Conference of Denominational Representatives," Philadelphia, February 16, 1907, p. 2. This report was found in the Industrial Immigration Work Box 1909-1930, YMCA Historical Library, New York City (hereafter cited as Immigration Box).

board the ships in transit, and after his arrival in the United States. The conference mapped out a two part program--for the immigrant in transit and in the cities. The YMCA representatives were to offer a seven point service for the immigrant in transit: (1) to contact the immigrant in his native home to prepare him for life in the United States; (2) to secure cooperation of YMCA and denominations in embarkation ports to help the immigrants; (3) to place uniformed agents at embarkation ports; (4) to appoint uniformed agents to accompany emigrants on board their vessels; (5) to distribute helpful literature throughout the process; (6) to prepare and forewarn Associations at points of destination within the United States; (7) to establish special branches of the YMCA at debarkation ports for the purpose of offering special services to the arriving immigrant. Once the immigrant arrived and settled, the conference envisioned continued YMCA service through the use of special branches of the Association for various ethnic groups which would provide recreational and religious services. Finally, the YMCA was to establish a multifaceted service program to include bureaus of information, employment, legal aid, medical aid, banking advice, as well as "improvement" courses in English, citizenship, naturalization procedures, Christian influence, sanitation, municipal law, housing conditions and "specially adapted literature."[31] Most of the program was to be studied more before put into operation. One exception was the immediate appointment of a YMCA agent for Ellis Island. The program recommended was both comprehensive and bold. If carried out, it would dwarf the longer established programs of the settlement houses. Because the YMCA was an international organization, it was uniquely equipped to make such a far-reaching program work.

By mid-April, 1907, a special advisory committee had been established to organize and coordinate the various phases of the immigration services. The complexity of the problems involved soon became apparent, and the Industrial Committee decided to hire a special secretary in charge of immigration work at home and abroad. On May 1, a conference of Association secretaries from all of the North Atlantic ports was convened to establish common programs in each city. The Industrial Committee appointed still another committee chaired by D. Chauncey Brewer of the Boston YMCA to begin work on the "specially adapted" literature for immigrants. All YMCA literature was to be cleared by Brewer's committee. D. Chauncey Brewer within a few months was to found the ultra-nationalist North America Civic League for Immigrants, a central function of which was to declare war on labor radicalism.[32] Among the members of the literature committee

---

[31]Ibid., pp. 3-5.

[32]"Industrial Committee Reports," May, 1907. The North American Civic League for Immigrants will be examined in more detail in the next chapter.

was Dr. Peter Roberts of Mahaney City, Pennsylvania, the man who would soon be named special secretary for Immigration Affairs. More than any other, Roberts would mold and develop the YMCA educational programs for foreigners.

The immigrant was likely to encounter a YMCA representative first at the port of embarkation. At the port, Association agents passed out pamphlets, set up comfort stations, and held religious services devoting not a little attention to wooing Catholics to Protestantism. Adam Scott, YMCA representative at Liverpool, England, asserted that "the greatest" service he rendered the emigrant was to "relate" him to the American YMCA. And Christian Phildius, general secretary of the World Committee, speaking before the Industrial Immigration Conference of 1910 boasted:

> Many of them [Italian immigrants] have embraced the Gospel News and tidings here, and going out as superstitious Roman Catholics have come back as Protestants (Hear, hear and applause). . . . In the province of Calabria, Sicily, a Protestant church has been established in a place called Salla, where 78 North American ex-immigrants from Italy have come back and have started a Protestant church. They went over as Roman Catholics, have heard the Gospel tidings and the Gospel News here and they came back and are now blessing in their own country (loud applause).[33]

A major ingredient in the foreign ports program was passing out literature and pamphlets. Pamphlets, often printed in as many as twenty-eight languages, carried religious instructions, introduction notices to YMCA workers in the United States, and practical and social advice. One card entitled "To Emigrants Going to America" advised the holder to report to the YMCA in America where "young men have the opportunity of fitting themselves for the requirements of American business life. . . ." Another entitled "YMCA Immigrant Guide Service--Ellis Island" advised immigrants to take the card "to the man with the Red Triangle [who will] assist you to the address of your relative in New York."[34] Assistance in finding local addresses

---

[33]Speech by Christian Phildius, *Industrial Immigration Conference of Representatives of the YMCA's in Europe and America* (Toronto: Thomas Bengough and Company, 1910), pp. 30-31, Immigration Box. This document is the complete proceedings of the conference and will be referred to hereafter as *Toronto Conference Proceedings*.

[34]Immigration Box. The languages in which the cards were printed were as follows: English, German, French, Italian, Dutch, Flemish, Swedish, Norwegian, Danish, Finnish, Russian, Polish, Bohemian, Hungarian, Romanian, Ruthenian, Bulgarian, Servian, Croatian,

was certainly welcomed by the confused and overwhelmed new arrivals, but there is some evidence that the card device was not very effective. One YMCA membership secretary complained:

> We find that the non-English speaking immigrants seldom present their cards of introduction but the English speaking men very generally do. . . . As to difficulties encountered by us. . . . We find some of the addresses given are of stores where the proprietor knows neither of the parties expecting to meet there and *very frequently* we find the men are at once hurried out of town to work.[35] [Italics mine]

Needless to say, if the card system did not work with the non-English speaking immigrants, then it was ineffective for the vast majority of immigrants. Furthermore, "very frequently" the service met with difficulty even for those English speaking immigrants who attempted to obtain YMCA help. Obviously, those immigrants unable to speak or understand English were the most befuddled and overawed by the chaos of Ellis Island and urban America. Unfortunately, these newcomers were least likely to get YMCA referral help.

YMCA representatives at the foreign ports also distributed much literature of potential value. One interesting handout was *A Catechism for Immigrants to the United States*. It explained suffrage laws, the public school system, child labor regulations and religious freedom. Also it attempted to inculcate those values and habits most rewarded in a corporate-industrial society. For example, it explained that "there are fortunes waiting for thousands upon thousands who are intelligent, industrious and frugal . . . there is no limit to the success that can be gained by labor, enterprise and thrift." The catechism also answered some important questions concerning management-labor relations. But the answers betrayed the bias of the "Zone of Agreement" policy, even in theory:

> Question. What are the best rules for me to follow?
> Answer. Be temperate; be faithful to your employer; give him an honest day's work and make sure you earn the liberal wages he pays you.
> Question. What have you to say about strikes?

Slovenian, Slovak, Lithuanian, Estonian, Lettish, Spanish, Armenian, Turkish, and Yiddish. Listed in *Toronto Conference Proceedings*, pp. 20-21.

[35] Letter from L. N. Logan, membership secretary of the Indianapolis YMCA to John R. McArthur of the New York City YMCA, n.d., Immigration Box.

Answer. Our country is afflicted with strikes
without number. If you are sure you are unjustly
treated by your employer, and have waited a long
time in vain for him to right the wrong, you have
the right to stop working for him. No one can
deny that simple right to you.
Question. Suppose he hires men to take the place
of the strikers?
Answer. He is quite likely to do that since his
own living depends upon keeping his mill or
factory going. Never forget that the man who
takes your place has the same rights that you
gave up, and it is a crime for you to molest or
to interfere in any way with him. Because so
many strikers have violated this law, rioting and
bloodshed have followed, and in almost every
instance the strikers have suffered punishment
for their wrong doing. Be very, very slow to
quit work or to strike, but, if you do so, do not
try to disturb in any way the man who takes your
place.

To a question on labor unions, the catechism warned that while they
might be necessary in rare instances, the worker must beware of their
inflamatory influence. "If you join a union," the catechism cautioned:

Make sure of never saying or doing anything
against your judgment, through the excited appeals of other members. Be moderate, slow and
thoughtful, and you cannot do a wiser and better
thing than to urge arbitration for any and all
troubles that may arise with your employer.[36]

The message to the immigrants was clear. Work hard, obey your boss,
don't be a complainer, and oppose labor activists. Certainly this
advice was more pleasing to management than labor.

YMCA agents also made their services available on board the
immigrant transport vessels. However, a number of obstacles again
limited their effectiveness. First, by the time the immigration
program became well organized, about 1909, many transport ships were
much faster and the journey from Europe to the United States was reduced to five days and nights. One day was taken up with vaccination and medical examination requirements. The first day was useless
because the immigrants were tired from the railroad journey to the
port, unpacking, and settling in their berths etc. Furthermore, in

---

[36] *A Catechism for Immigrants to the United States* (place not given: publisher not given, n.d.), pp. 20-22, Immigration Box. This booklet was probably published by the YMCA *Circa* 1910.

the fall, the ships were crowded with returnees--that is immigrants who had returned to Europe for the summer. These foreigners were already familiar with the United States, did not have to be reprocessed through Ellis Island, and thus did not respond well to YMCA programs. Nonetheless, the Association agents took advantage of every opportunity to appear before the immigrants to lead song fests and give stereotopicon lectures on Ellis Island, YMCA facilities and other subjects. The agents also distributed literature, YMCA cards, and railroad maps of the United States, as well as candy to the children. But a central underlying motivation of all of these services was to recruit members for the YMCA. As a YMCA agent aboard the *S.S. Lusitania* put it "the YMCA was quietly but persistently kept before the gathering." He later volunteered to lead a band concert on board ship and boasted in his report "This brought me before the crowd three nights in succession."[37]

Limitations on the agent's objectives were also inherent in the YMCA's relationship with the ship owner. The YMCA was dependent upon the largess of the shipping companies for allowing them on board at all. Thus, the problems resulting from the immigrants' poor treatment aboard the vessel were beyond the agents' capabilities. No matter how concerned the agent may have been about the discomfort, filth, and harrassment which immigrants faced on board ship, he could do little because of his dependence on the shipping company.

One agent, identified only as Mr. James, described the hardships of a steerage trip on the *S.S. Batavia*. His tale was one long horror story. Fresh water for the steerage was non-existent which meant that the unhappy immigrants were forced to wash themselves, their clothing, and their greasy dishes in cold sea water. The toilets were small and far too few. Day and night, long lines of steerage waited for their use. One woman, James reported with revulsion, "was seen coming from a washroom with excrement on her feet." Only eight stewards and three stewardesses were on duty to serve 15,000 passengers. The stewards drank heavily and were often drunk. Two sailors fought each other with knives over trying to sleep with women passengers. The staff smuggled whiskey on board and sold it at exhorbitant prices to the passengers. Female passengers were harrassed to the extent that "No single female was free from the vulgarity of the crew." In return for their favors, the women would receive "a meal from the cook or a bottle of wine from a fireman." In all fairness to the crew

---

[37]The above account was based on a report by John Sumner, European Emigration Secretary, who described his role as YMCA agent aboard the *S.S. Lusitania*, September 13-19, 1913. Immigration Box. The list of his equipment indicates the kind of services he was able to render: "portable stereotopicon and four sets of slides, gramaphone and seventy records, games, song books, hymn books, illustrated magazines, letter paper and envelopes, railroad maps and Association Immigration cards."

members, however, James admitted that some of the women invited their attention. Signs were conspicuously placed warning the steerage not to spit on the floor because of the danger of consumption. Yet James complained that "no receptacles, whether spitoons or slop buckets were provided. The filth below decks must have been nearly intolerable because only once during a seventeen day journey was the steerage area washed. Mr. James himself, incidentally, bribed an officer to allow him to sleep in his room. During the two and one-half week ordeal, the only complaint Mr. James made concerned a deckhand's obscenity to two young girls. He made a number of recommendations to his superior whose lame reaction was "Some of the recommendations of Mr. James are in force on some liners, notably relating to the State Room on one and to liquor on another."[38]

    Clearly, YMCA representatives were afraid to agitate on these problems for the same reason that they could not agitate on certain social issues in the United States. They could not afford to antagonize their benefactors. If Association agents championed humane treatment of steerage, the shipowners would have simply refused to allow the agents on board. The most that one can say about the YMCA agent in transit is that with his stereotopicon lectures, song fests, and handouts, he probably made a little more endurable a most unpleasant experience. But beyond that, the Association probably failed miserably in addressing itself to the immediate needs of the abused transients.

    The next important point of contact between the YMCA and the immigrant was at the debarkation port, usually New York and the formidable Ellis Island. Here, the immigrant was sorely in need of help. The number of inspections, interrogations, rejections and quarantines must have produced reactions ranging from despair to hysteria. Upon entering the New York harbor, an American pilot steered the ship into Ellis Island where it was immediately quarantined until examined by New York health officers. Next the Public Health and Marine Service of the United States Treasury provided a medical staff which conducted an immigrant-by-immigrant health inspection. Then the ship was boarded by the United States Customs officials and by representatives of the Boarding Division of the Department of Immigration consisting of Inspectors, Doctors, and Boarding Matrons. The immigrant had to pass the medical inspection first. If he was suspected of any contagious disease he was held for special inquiry which meant detention at the hospital at Ellis Island until cured, at which time he could be further processed, or if not cured,

---

[38] E. S. Towson, "Report of an Investigation Made At New York Concerning Arriving Immigrants," (July, 1907), pp. 22-24, Immigration Box. Hereafter cited as "Towson Report." James had made a number of recommendations to improve conditions for the steerage passengers. Among them were that no liquor be allowed to crew or passengers and that steerage passengers be permitted the use of the staterooms.

deported. The immigrants knew from the grapevine that one must avoid being "S.I.'d." (Special Inspection).

If an immigrant passed medical inspection, or was later cured of disease, he had to face the customs inspector. The inspector had a copy of the ship's manifest which included a dossier on each passenger emigrating to the United States. First cabin immigrants (those traveling first class) were the subject of "perfunctory" questioning, but for second class and steerage passengers, the questioning could be probing indeed. The inspector had a list of twenty-nine questions by which he could double-check information in the manifest in search of inconsistencies. He was particularly careful in questioning about contract laborers. If the passenger answered all questions satisfactorily, he was ushered into another room to declare his luggage and have it inspected. After this, the immigrant, if not "S.I.'d" was admitted. Females, however, were subjected to the further harrassment of being "spotted" by one of the boarding matrons as a prostitute. One must marvel at the omniscience of the matron who could detect a prostitute on sight! Of course, at any point along this inspection line an alien might be "S.I.'d" by the doctor, the customs inspector, the interrogator or the matron.

Perhaps the most debasing part of the Ellis Island gruel was the medical inspection. During this ordeal an alien might be "S.I.'d" as a mental defective because of "family quarrels" in which case the doctor chalked an "X" on his shoulder and assigned him to a "cage" for special examination. If the immigrant escaped designation as a mental risk, another doctor might brand him with any of several symbols for physical disorders--"G" for goetre, "H" for hernia, "S" for spine disease etc. Any of these markings sent the immigrant to the special inspection which in turn either admitted him to the Ellis Island hospital or returned him to the normal processing line. The hospital reserved the option of recommending patients for further processing or deportation.

The processee fortunate enough to avoid a doctor's brand was forwarded to "the line" where he was categorized by a "grouper" for further interrogation. If he failed to answer the questions properly or if he revealed inconsistencies with his written records, the interrogator could again designate him "S.I." If not, he was allowed to convert his foreign currency for dollars, and was marched through the maze of corridors to the railroad station or steamer dock. There, for the first time, was he likely to meet a YMCA representative passing out pamphlets.[39]

---

[39] The quotation as well as the entire account of the Ellis Island procedures is based on a fascinating eye-witness report included in the "Towson Report," pp. 1-9. The complete report, running to twenty-nine single-spaced typed pages, in addition to the Ellis Island account, includes reports on the independent agencies at work on Ellis Island, detention house work, the James report cited above, and special YMCA work for English speaking immigrants. Parts of the report are included in the appendix.

The immigrant passing through this maddening introduction to life in the United States must soon have feared that the bureaucracy had total power over his life. On the other hand, he surely must have developed a grapevine knowledge of what answers *not* to give the inspectors, how *not* to attract the matron's attention and what *not* to bring into the country. Nonetheless, the immigrant desperately needed help during the Ellis Island sojourn and the YMCA did not provide it until the immigrant had somehow passed inspection. Realizing these shortcomings, E. S. Towson, in charge of YMCA operations at Ellis Island, recommended that the Association agent offer help to those immigrants who ran afoul of the inspection machinery. His reasoning, however, was self-serving. "The point is this" he urged, "a man detained or in danger of exclusion is inclined to be more grateful to the YMCA than, when free to depart, [he] merely receives a card of introduction in the railroad rooms."[40] Towson's statement, besides questionable motivation, revealed that throughout the entire inspection ordeal, the first time an immigrant met a YMCA representative was when he pressed a wallet-sized introduction card into his hand as he awaited the train to his destination. As with the in-transit program, the YMCA did not meet the immediate needs of the unhappy processees at Ellis Island. Thus, from the time the emigrant left his port of embarkation until he finished the trying procedures at Ellis Island, he received only limited aid and comfort from the YMCA. This was understandable. An orderly and efficient program was virtually impossible given the chaos of the European ports, the travails of the journey, and the imposing human machinery of Ellis Island. Moreover, not until they settled and obtained jobs did the immigrants become a recognizable segment of the urban community and its problems. In short, the problems which the emigrant faced were transitory; the problems of the ghetto-dwelling immigrant were not. He had to learn a new language, become accustomed to a whole list of political, judicial, and social customs, and become initiated into the wiles of the corporate industrial state. He had to be "Americanized." To this end, the YMCA organized a far-reaching program headed by an amazingly energetic man who preferred to be called "Peter Roberts (Ph.D.)."

---

[40]*Ibid.*, p. 8. It is impossible to say whether or not Towson's recommendations for a wider-ranging YMCA program at Ellis Island were acted upon. There were no further reports in the Immigration Box.

CHAPTER V

PETER ROBERTS: THE TRAVAILS OF A MODERATE

> "The object of the lesson should be not only to teach English, but also to raise the standard of living by suggestion. Mention is made in later lessons of 'piano,' 'music,' 'parlor,' 'a clean house,' etc., all of which may appear inappropriate in view of the way many of these people live."[1]
>   Peter Roberts

> "The 'political boss' is a term generally applied to master politicians who are corrupt, tyrannical and unscrupulous."[2]
>   Peter Roberts
>   *Civics for Coming Americans*

> "Now immigrants are young men, but if they were marched directly to our homelike buildings, they would not only soil and disfigure them, but they would, by their entry en masse, defeat Association purposes, since they would not only pollute the physical, but the moral atmosphere."[3]
>   YMCA Executive

---

[1] Peter Roberts, "The Roberts Method of Teaching English to Foreigners," *Bulletin No. 3*, Illinois Miners and Mechanics Institute (Urbana: University of Illinois Press, 1914), p. 41.

[2] Peter Roberts, *Civics for Coming Americans* (New York: Association Press, 1917), p. 100.

[3] Speech by D. Chauncey Brewer in "Conference on Work with Immigrants," Boston, December 10, 1909, p. 3. Industrial Immigration Work Box 1909-1930, YMCA Historical Library, New York City.

> "Be temperate; be faithful to your employer; give him an honest day's work and make sure you earn the liberal wages he pays you."[4]
>
> Advice printed in
> YMCA handout

> "The contents of the textbooks in use [for a YMCA English for foreigners course] exhorted the workers to love and honor the boss and to obey the foreman as if he were Jehovah himself . . . the sort of humiliating tripe which was bound to alienate any workman with a trace of character and independence."[5]
>
> Norbert Wiener
> Jewish observer

By the time Peter Roberts became immigration secretary of the Industrial Committee on July 1, 1907, he had already established himself as an expert on immigration. He had spent considerable time among the anthracite coal miners in his native Pennsylvania, had worked among immigrants in the Association railroad program in various parts of the country, and had written a well-received book entitled *Anthracite Coal Communities*.[6] As immigration secretary, Roberts soon developed a wide-ranging educational program for immigrants including a sequence of courses in English, civics, and history. He wrote all of his own textbooks, even a songbook for immigrants, and

---

[4] *A Catechism for Immigrants to the United States* (place not given: publisher not given, n.d.), p. 20. Immigration Box. Probably published circa 1910.

[5] Norbert Wiener, *Ex Prodigy - My Childhood and Youth* (New York: Simon & Schuster, 1953), pp. 266-67.

[6] "Biographical Data Sheet" provided to the author by Virginia Downes, Head Librarian, YMCA Historical Library, New York City. Also, Gerd Korman, *Industrialization Immigrants and Americanizers* (Madison, Wisconsin: The State Historical Society of Wisconsin, 1967), pp. 141-43. Edith Terry Bremer "Development of Private Social Work with the Foreign Born," *Annals of the American Academy of Political and Social Science*, CCLVII (March, 1949), p. 140, and "Foreign Community and Immigration Work of the National Young Women's Christian Association" *The Immigrant in America Review*, I (January, 1916), pp. 73-82.

distributed them throughout the country billed as "The Roberts' Method" for teaching foreigners. He traveled from coast to coast visiting corporations, school boards, church groups, and even prisons, demonstrating the Roberts' Method, emphasizing its adaptability to business needs, and enhancing his reputation. One of his most impressive demonstrations involved bringing immigrants in off the street who could neither speak nor understand English and having them master the first lesson within an hour or so.[7]

Roberts divided his English lessons into three series: domestic, industrial and commercial. In each series he built his lessons around the practical, everyday experiences of the immigrant. For example, the first lesson of the domestic series, which he used to demonstrate his method, was centered around waking up in the morning. With each sentence, Roberts would act out the action involved, practically undressing himself to the tittering delight of all watching. The wake-up lesson went like this:

awake	I awake from sleep.
open	I open my eyes.
look	I look for my watch.
find	I find my watch.
see	I see what time it is.
is	It is six o'clock.
must get up	I must get up.
throw back	I throw back the bed clothes
get out	I get out of bed.
put on	I put on my pants.
put on	I put on my stockings and shoes.
wash	I wash myself.
comb	I comb my hair.
put on	I put on my collar and necktie.
put on	I put on my vest and coat.
open	I open the door of my bedroom.
go down	I go down stairs.

---

[7] Peter Roberts, "The Roberts Method of Teaching English to Foreigners," *Bulletin No. 3*, Illinois Miners and Mechanics Institute (Urbana: University of Illinois Press, 1914), pp. 37-40; also Peter Roberts, "The YMCA Teaching Foreign Speaking Men," *The Immigrants in America Review*, I (June, 1915), pp. 18-23; and "The YMCA Among the Immigrants," *Survey*, XXIX (February 15, 1913), pp. 697-700. See also Edward A. Halsey, "Our Brothers the Immigrants," *The World Today*, XIX (December, 1910), pp. 1375-81.

Series "A," Domestic, involved the following lessons on the same order as the one above.

1. Getting up in the morning.
2. Getting wood to light the fire.
3. Lighting the fire.
4. Preparing breakfast.
5. Table utensils.
6. Eating breakfast.
7. The man washing.
8. A family of eight.
9. Welcoming a visitor.
10. Going to bed.

Series "B," Industrial, included:

1. Going to work.
2. Beginning the day's work.
3. Shining shoes.
4. The miner going to work.
5. The railroad laborer at work.
6. The laborer in the steel works.
7. A man looking for work.
8. Quitting a job.
9. A man injured.
10. Finishing the day's work.

Series "C," Commercial, included:

1. Writing a letter.
2. Buying and using stamps.
3. Going to the station for a railroad ticket.
4. Taking the train to New Haven.
5. Pay day.
6. Home expenses.
7. Buying a hat.
8. Taking money to the bank.
9. Sending money home.
10. Buying a lot and building a house.

Roberts thus succeeded in building each of his beginning English lessons around an experience common to most immigrants. His acting was rather "hammy" to the delight of his pupils, and within a short while he had trained hundreds of volunteer teachers in his method.[8]

---

[8] *Ibid.*, pp. 39-40. Roberts explained his technique in two interesting and detailed teaching manuals: *English for Coming Americans, Teacher's Aids* (New York: Association Press, 1912) and

A man of incessant activity and indefatigable energy, Roberts not only developed and revised his program and texts, he also promoted them with vigor as well. Copyrighting his system in 1908, he sold his method to numerous public and private schools. In November, 1908, alone, he traveled and lectured his way through Indiana, Illinois, and Ohio holding institutes and seminars such as the five-day program at Troy, New York. In January and February, 1909, Roberts enrolled over 1,600 immigrants in his English program and in March, he opened eight centers for teaching English in New York City alone.[9] In April, 1910, he introduced his system at Sing Sing and Western Penitentiary in Pennsylvania. By June, 1910, enrollment had doubled in a year to 9,000 immigrants. By May, 1911, that figure had jumped to 12,000 and one month later, to 13,000.[10]

As his program grew, Roberts' value to the YMCA grew also. He started out in 1907 with a salary of $1800 per year. That was raised to $2000 plus $1350 expenses in 1908 and the next year, Roberts was making $5000 with an expense account of $1500.[11] None of this included royalties on the substantial sales of his many textbooks.

Most of Roberts' promotional effort was geared toward industry which in part explains his increasing value to the Association. He offered to set up a program for industry to teach English to foreign workers during the noon hour and to tailor his "message" to the desires of industry. Thus, by late 1910, Scranton, Pittsburgh, and Wilmerding, Pennsylvania as well as Cleveland and Chicago had full-time immigration secretaries paid by local business to serve foreigners. Boston, Philadelphia, Milwaukee and Duluth followed shortly afterward. In November, 1911, lumber interests hired YMCA English teachers to serve foreign speaking lumberjacks in Maine. And in early 1914, the Ford Motor Company hired the YMCA to inaugurate an English program among its 15,000 workers, 85% of whom were foreign born. Ford paid the "entire salary" of the Association secretary.[12]

English for Coming Canadians, Teacher's Manual (New York: Association Press, 1912).

[9]"Industrial Committee Reports," December, 1908, February, March and April, 1909.

[10]*Ibid.*, February, 1910, May and June, 1911.

[11]*Ibid.*, January, 1909, February, 1910.

[12]*Ibid.*, October, 1910, November, 1911, April, 1914, and February, 1915.

The primary purpose of the English programs established by industry was to inculcate habits of safety among the foreign worker. Obviously, industry had difficulty with those workers who could not understand English because they could not easily follow directions, were harder to train, and presented an added safety hazard. But most industries did not allow Roberts to use the programs he developed. Instead they demanded that he fit his program to their particular needs, that is, to teach safety habits applicable to their job.

United States Steel Company, for example, established a YMCA Roberts Method program in 1913. A typical lesson in the tailor-made Roberts English went like this.

LESSON II

Start work	I go to the Mill to start work.
Clock house	First I go to the Clock House.
Card rack	I take my number card from the CARD RACK.
Go	I go to the CLOCK.
Put	I put my CARD in the CLOCK.
Ring	I RING the CLOCK.
Shows	The clock shows the TIME I START TO WORK.
Sign	I see A SIGN ON THE CLOCK HOUSE.
Safety rules	It reads I MUST KNOW THE SAFETY RULES.
Think	I think of the LITTLE RULE BOOK.
Was given	It was given at the Employment Office.
Must read	I MUST READ THE RULE BOOK.
Safety rules	I WANT TO KNOW ALL OF THE SAFETY RULES.
Do not want	I do not want to get hurt.
Be careful	I will be careful not to hurt the other men.
Leave	I leave the CLOCK HOUSE for my work.
Roadway	I GO BY THE ROADWAY.
Not run across	I DO NOT RUN ACROSS THE RAILROAD YARDS.
Might be struck	I MIGHT BE STRUCK BY A TRAIN OF CARS.
Look both ways	When I cross a railroad track I look both ways.
Train coming	I see if there is a train coming.
Is clear	THE WAY IS CLEAR--THERE IS NOTHING COMING ON THE TRACK.
Cross	I cross the track on the roadway.
Arrive	I arrive at my place of work.
Must not climb	I must not climb over the MACHINERY.
Go by	I GO BY THE PASSAGEWAYS THERE.
Use the stairs	I USE THE STAIRS WHICH ARE OVER THE MACHINERY.[13]

---

[13]United States Steel Corporation, "Lessons for Teaching Foreigners English by the Roberts Method in Use by the YMCA Teachers in Our Mill Districts," *Bulletin No. 4* (November, 1913), p. 8, Immigration Box. An excellent example of the enthusiasm generated within the industrial leadership by the Roberts Method can be found in G. W. Tupper, "The Efficiency of Mill Operatives," pamphlet found in the Immigration Box.

In like manner, when the YMCA began teaching English to foreign workers of International Harvester in 1911, the main thrust of the program was to make them efficient and obedient. One of the lessons was designed to inculcate habits of punctuality and discipline:

I hear the whistle. I must hurry.
I hear the five minute whistle.
It is time to go into the shop.
I take my check for the gate board
    and hang it on the department board.
I change my clothes and get ready to work.
The starting whistle blows.
I eat my lunch.
It is forbidden to eat until then.
The whistle blows at five minutes of
    starting time.
I get ready to go to work.
I work until the whistle blows to
    quit.
I leave my place nice and clean.
I put all my clothes in my locker.
I go home.[14]

Other lessons given under industry's auspices covered efficiency in various jobs, safety rules for machinery, and what to do in case of injury or accident. U.S. Steel presented a lesson which emphasized the importance of obtaining company treatment.

May fly	A chip may fly and injure me.
Small cut	I have a small cut on my hand.
Must tell	I must tell the FOREMAN.
To hospital	I must GO TO THE HOSPITAL.
Must be treated	The injury must be treated.
Poisoned	It may become poisoned.
Will cure	The Doctor at the HOSPITAL will cure my hand.
Injury	The injury will not be very bad.
Go back	I will be able to go back to work.
Pay me	The company will pay me while I go to the HOSPITAL.
To the hospital	THE COMPANY WANTS ME TO GO TO THE HOSPITAL WITH EVERY LITTLE INJURY.
Have trouble	I WILL NOT HAVE TROUBLE WITH THE INJURIES.
Little injury	A LITTLE INJURY MAY BE A BIG ONE.
Must dress	THE DOCTOR MUST DRESS MY INJURIES.

---

[14]*Harvester World*, III (March, 1912), p. 31 quoted in Korman, *Immigrants and Americanizers*, pp. 144-45.

The International Harvester added the warning:

> No benefits will be paid if you are hurt
> while scuffing [*sic*] or fooling.
> No benefits will be paid if you are hurt
> or get sick as a result of having been
> drinking.[15]

Thus the Roberts English program, industrial style, centered around one aspect only of immigrant life, the job. The YMCA, although equipped with a much broader program, was practically helpless to combat the narrower business approach. The English program, however well-intentioned, was molded and controlled by the business benefactors who paid for the teachers, provided the facilities and donated to the Association. Never was the adage more appropriate "He who pays the piper calls the tune."

The beginning English program, because of the wide sponsorship of industry, became largely subverted to industrial ends. But the program was much broader than that, and Roberts never lost sight of the secondary goal of helping immigrants to deal with the everyday problems which arose in American urban life. He designed the commercial series, for example, to help combat the everyday exploitation to which immigrants fell victim. The lesson on "taking a train" explained to the foreigner that the policeman was the best guide when directions were needed and that he must take care to keep the receipt for his baggage. The lesson on "pay day" instructed the immigrant how to correct errors in the pay envelope, and how much coal, rent and groceries should cost. Other lessons involved tips on buying clothes, mailing letters, sending money to the folks back home, depositing money in the bank, and buying a lot and home. All of this advice concerned incidents that all immigrants faced at one time or another and was both well-intentioned and practical.[16]

But there was another message, more subtle perhaps, in the Roberts English program. Roberts wanted to provide lessons which would help immigrants to think, act, dress and adopt the life style of middle class Americans. He shared the view of many educators, social workers and settlement house volunteers that his efforts ought to further the process of Americanization.

To be sure, Roberts' brand of assimilation could scarcely be characterized as militantly nationalistic. In fact, his method of cultural attrition was almost subliminal. Concerning immigrant dress

---

[15] U.S. Steel, *Bulletin No. 4*, p. 8. Korman, *Immigrants and Americanizers*, p. 146.

[16] All of these lessons were printed on drill cards found in several boxes of Roberts Method materials at the YMCA Historical Library, New York City. The lessons are included in the appendix.

and life style he said:

> Another objection has been made that "The foreigner does not wear a collar and tie." This may be true, but the nearer he approaches the American standard the surer he is of doing so. The object of the lesson should be not only to teach English but also to raise the standard of living by suggestion. Mention is made in later lessons of "piano," "music," "parlor," "a clean house," etc., all of which may appear inappropriate in view of the way many of these people live. But as the effort should be to help the men to a higher standard of living, these suggestions are not only justified but beneficial.[17]

Roberts' "soft" approach to Americanization was based on his belief that immigrants would reflect the standards of the society which they experienced. Thus, if through education, they were exposed to "the right ideas, right moral values, right political concepts and examples of justice, purity, liberty and freedom,"[18] they would themselves absorb these values. To Roberts, the YMCA provided the proper environment and the Roberts Method the right cultural influence.

Roberts had vehicles other than his beginning English course to convey his version of Americanism. In his advanced English, he used extensive readings, carefully chosen from such impeccably patriotic sources as the Daughters of the American Revolution and the North American Civic League for Immigrants. Some of the readings may have been strongly suggested to him by the literature committee through which all selections had to be cleared.[19]

Some of the advanced English readings were designed to emphasize the benevolence of American industry and the sky-is-the-limit concept of opportunity in America. Two stories in the advanced course, for example, told of a delighted immigrant who worked for a kind-hearted boss at the U.S. Steel Corporation. "Boss Brown treats his men right, and he expects his men to treat him right," the lesson read. The story also told of a poor immigrant who lost his job because he "thought he could get good money and loaf on the job." Another story told of a benevolent foreman who helped an immigrant

---

[17]Peter Roberts, "The Roberts Method. . . ."*Bulletin No. 3,* p. 41.

[18]Peter Roberts, "The Ethnic Factors in Immigrants to North America," *ibid.,* p. 28.

[19]Korman, *Immigrants and Americanizers,* p. 142. "Industrial Committee Reports," April, 1907.

worker to "buy some shares in a Building and Loan" and thus enabled him to buy a lot for $240 and build a home for $1,257. The gleeful immigrant boasted at the end, "Now the $12 a month rent we used to pay, as well as all we can save, goes into that house, and in a few years more it will be clear. I am very grateful to the foreman for the idea that I could save if I made up my mind to do so."[20]

Other lessons in the advanced English courses drummed home the idea that immigrants had entered the land of rags-to-riches. One such lesson, for example, explained that immigrants had prospered marvelously in the United States because they were "willing to work hard, to obey the laws of the land." Of course, the United States welcomed all immigrants of "good moral character" and provided them with "greater freedom, more happiness and larger chances of success" than ever they had in Europe. In return for these blessings, the lesson advised that the immigrant show his gratitude "by giving what is best in him to the country."[21]

In his textbook *Civics for Coming Americans*, Roberts explained to the immigrant the workings of the two party system, voting procedures, the primary system, and the basics of American history. Here too he took the opportunity to reenforce political orthodoxy and to attack that menace to all goodness and honesty, the political boss. Written in question and answer format, the textbook defined political bosses as, "master politicians who are corrupt, tyrannical, and unscrupulous." Acknowledging that the bosses were shrewd and farsighted, *Civics for Coming Americans* nevertheless warned that "invariably such men win office for private and selfish interests, and the people's business is neglected." The book described the political machine as the bosses' "clansmen" who run the party in their own interests and who come to power because of the indifference of the voters. It predicted that the machine would be ruined when the voters were "alert, intelligent, and demand good men in office." Occasionally, one answer explained, popular outrage against the machine's corruption effected a temporary check on its operations. But when the fervor subsided, it pessimistically observed, "soon the machine is again in control."[22]

Whether subtle or not, Roberts' prescription for Americanization was far less harsh than that advocated by a powerful group of

---

[20] Peter Roberts, *English Reading Lessons* (New York: YMCA Industrial Department, 1917), pp. 14-16.

[21] Peter Roberts, *English for Coming Americans, Advanced Course, First Reader* (New York: Association Press, 1918), 14th edition, p. 78.

[22] Peter Roberts, *Civics for Coming Americans* (New York: Association Press, 1917), p. 100.

militant nationalists in the YMCA leadership. Led by many of the old guard Association secretaries, particularly the Boston group, these ardent Americanizers saw immigrants primarily as a threat to the values and institutions of their social group. To them, the goal of the YMCA education effort was to root out radicalism of any kind except an uncritical love of country.

The militant Boston group was led by George W. Mehaffey, general secretary of the Boston YMCA, Arthur Stoddard Johnson, former general secretary, and D. Chauncey Brewer, chairman of the literature committee which screened Roberts' selections. In 1907, these three founded the North American Civic League for Immigrants under the auspices of the Boston YMCA. Several months later they made the N.A.C.L. a separate entity, but maintained the closest cooperation with the YMCA.[23] In the words of one of its founders, the

---

[23] William B. Whiteside, *The Boston YMCA and the Community Need - A Century's Evolution 1851-1951* (New York: Association Press, 1951), pp. 153-54. Also "Conference on Work With Immigrants," Boston, December 10, 1909, p. 3, Immigration Box (hereafter cited as "Boston Immigration Conference"). Also "Industrial Committee Reports," annual summary report, 1908. D. Chauncey Brewer, "A Patriotic Movement for the Assimilation of Immigrants', *Editorial Review*, III (Aug. 1910), pp. 786-800. See also, North American Civic League for Immigrants, *Annual Report*, 1910-1911, p. 9. Officers and members of the League were: D. Chauncey Brewer, lawyer and civic leader, and active in the Boston Chamber of Commerce, president; Bernard J. Rothwell, industrialist and president of the Boston Chamber of Commerce, vice-president; Francis B. Sears, treasurer. Board of Managers: Nathan L. Amster, Jacob P. Bates, Lucius Tuttle, president of the Boston & Maine Railroad, Samuel B. Capen, officer and director of Torrey, Brighton, & Capen Co., Edward H. Haskell, president of the Haskell-Dawes Machine Co., and the American Rotary Power Co., Richard C. Humphreys, Arthur S. Johnson, president of the Boston YMCA, the Rt. Rev. William Lawrence, William E. Murdock, Bernard J. Rothwell, the Most Rev. William H. O'Connell, William T. Rich, and the officers of the league, all of Boston. Non-Boston members included: Frank A. Vanderlip, president of the National City Bank of New York City; Thomas M. Mulry, Jacob A. Riis, Felix Warburg, prominent banker and philanthropist, and Robert Watchorn of New York City; James Cardinal Gibbons, Charles England, president of the Baltimore Chamber of Commerce, and Jacob H. Hollander, economist and financial advisor, of Baltimore; Clinton R. Woodruff, lawyer and member of the Pennsylvania legislature, and William R. Tucker, secretary of the Philadelphia National Board of Trade, of Philadelphia. Later members included E. J. Buffington, president of the Illinois Steel Company, L. Wilbur Messer, general secretary of the Chicago YMCA, George E. Roberts, and John F. Smulski, immigrant banker, president of the Northwestern Trust and Savings Bank, and vice-president of the Chicago Chamber of Commerce, of Chicago; Charles H. Pugh, financier, and John Wanamaker, prominent merchant of Philadelphia. Cited in

N.A.C.L. was "a patriotic organization" established to aid the immigrant "to greater industrial efficiency, to better comprehension of the rights and privileges of American citizenship, to make him a loyal, patriotic citizen, and to give him a clean appreciation of Christian manhood."[24]

In reality, however, the N.A.C.L. was contemptuous of the immigrant and fearful of his threat to American institutions. One pamphlet the N.A.C.L. distributed complained that the "tide [of immigrants] is increasing . . . we have reached the saturation point." Another warned that "our institutions are imperilled by the influx of great numbers of people--speaking different languages: unacquainted with democratic theories of government and whose sympathies are alienated by those who prey upon them."[25]

N.A.C.L. president, D. Chauncey Brewer, openly expressed the contempt and condescension with which his organization approached the immigrant. Addressing the Boston YMCA membership in 1909, Brewer supported the general YMCA goal of creating "centers of healthful influence for young men." But he objected vigorously to opening YMCA doors to the dregs of Europe. "If they are marched in directly to our homelike buildings," Brewer thundered, "they would not only soil and disfigure them, but they would, . . . pollute the physical and the moral atmosphere." He advocated the establishment of segregated rooms for immigrants in their own communities where they could be used "without embarrassing the central administration in its larger work." The distasteful alternative would have been to set aside special areas of the established "Y's" equipped with "information bureaus adapted to the use of peasants." To Brewer, such a solution was unacceptable because YMCA work "must be limited to the reception and ennobling of men who have become neat and respectable in their person and attire." The YMCA, Brewer warned, must not be allowed to lose its "proper ethical and religious" perspective by cluttering itself with special programs for "the raw product" from Europe. He believed most immigrants to be beneath the reach of the "Y's" helping hand. They were "raw crass things" he hissed, "their eyes are dull--physically they are fit, but mentally and spiritually

---

Edward George Hartmann, *The Movement to Americanize the Immigrant* (New York: Columbia University Press, 1948), pp. 38-39ff.

[24]"Boston Immigration Conference," p. 3.

[25]North American Civic League for Immigrants, Pamphlets (*circa* 1909), Immigration Box. The Boston YMCA cooperated with the Rhode Island Associations in publishing and distributing pamphlets of a similar alarmist nature. One concluded, "Patriotism calls us to immediate action in every industrial community towards assimilating these new Americans to Rhode Island."

asleep." Brewer concluded his address with the ominous warning that the American people faced "the greatest crisis that a free people was ever called upon to meet." He called the YMCA membership to its "patriotic duty . . . immigrants upon immigrants are to be directed, taught, succored, led to a just appreciation of our institutions."[26]

But whatever its intentions to teach and succor, the N.A.C.L. did a great deal more harrassing and haranguing of the immigrant. Frightened into believing that its most hysterical fears about the immigrant were well founded, the N.A.C.L. responded to I.W.W. activity in Massachusetts, for example, by arming itself for Armageddon against radicalism. The N.A.C.L. report of 1913-1914 suggested the extent to which anti-radicalism had gripped the organization. In Cambridge, N.A.C.L. secretaries combated "foreigners under radical influence." At Waterburg, the League, by its "constructive work," forced the I.W.W. to leave. In Philadelphia, after a six-month campaign against the I.W.W., "the League won the confidence of large numbers" of immigrants. At Lynn, the League moved to calm disorders in a shoe factory, and at Peabody, N.A.C.L. agents "engaged in constructive work" to counteract "threatening conditions." Local industry, quickly came to view the N.A.C.L. as the troubleshooting, deradicalizing arm of the YMCA.[27]

To Brewer and the N.A.C.L., the mirror image of anti-radicalism was unquestioning patriotism. Thus, while the league busied itself combating socialists, I.W.W. spokesmen, and other assorted radicals, it also developed a reservoir of literature designed to promote an emotional love of country. One handout entitled "I Am An American" consisted of two paragraphs. The first, "The Native American," concluded:

> My forefathers were America in the making; they spoke in her council halls; they died on her battlefields; they commanded her ships; they cleared her forests. Dawns reddened and paled. Staunch hearts of mine beat fast at each new star in the nation's flag. Keen eyes of mine foresaw her greater glory; the sweep of her seas, the plenty of her plains, the man-hives in her billionwired cities. Every drop of blood in me holds a heritage of patriotism. I am proud of my past. I am an American.

---

[26] "Boston Immigration Conference," pp. 4-5.

[27] North American Civic League for Immigrants, *Annual Report 1913-1914* (Boston: N.A.C.L., 1914), pp. 4-6. Business response cited, p. 14. Other sketches of the League appear in Korman, *Immigrants and Americanizers*, pp. 148-49, and Hartmann, *The Movement to Americanize the Immigrant*, pp. 90-97, and Chapter 2.

The second, "The Naturalized American," ended with these stirring words:

> The history of my ancestors is a trail of blood to the palace gate of the czar. But then the dream came--the dream of America. In the light of Liberty's torch the atom of dust became a man and the straw in the wind became a woman for the first time. "See," said my father, pointing to the flag that fluttered near, "that flag of stars and stripes is yours; it is the emblem of the promised land. It means the hope of humanity. Live for it; die for it." Under the open sky of my new country I swore to do so, and every drop of blood in me will keep that vow. I am proud of my future. I am an American.[28]

Other league pamphlets were considerably more elaborate than "I Am An American." One continued for eighteen pages and contained four "messages" driving home such themes as the importance of communicating in English, the necessity for staunch loyalty to the new nation, and the lessons of the life of Abraham Lincoln. One message on the history of the United States told how freedom conquered tyranny in the American revolution, how opportunity was unbound for those who, like the pioneers, were "industrious, frugal, honest, and brave," and how the immigrant could "easily understand" how noble men might differently interpret the Constitution and therefore wage civil war.[29]

Thus, the N.A.C.L. tried to convince the immigrant that in this land of unlimited opportunity, freedom, and justice, prosperity could be his were he only to think, act, and live like an American. In the process, of course, he should give his undivided allegiance to his new flag and join the battle against those who did not. Clearly, the strident tones of Americanization, N.A.C.L. style, constituted an important force within the general structure of the YMCA immigration program. N.A.C.L. and YMCA leadership cross fertilized each other and in fact were often indistinguishable. All of the reading selections chosen by the more moderate Peter Roberts had to be approved by the literature committee of D. Chauncey Brewer which meant that much of the subtlety envisioned by Roberts became well-mixed with the N.A.C.L. brand of assimilation. Thus, much of the Roberts program became indistinguishable from that of those more militant who sought primarily to convert alienation into allegiance.

---

[28] Pamphlet, Immigration Box.

[29] North American Civic League for Immigrants, *Messages for New Comers to the United States* (Boston: N.A.C.L., n.d.), Immigration Box.

The influence of the militant nationalists was readily apparent in the Roberts advanced English course. The readings included numerous selections on historical, patriotic themes, particularly civil war or revolutionary settings. There were also many excerpts from emotional sources such as the following from Newell Dwight Hillis:

> If possible, their patriotism is more intense than that of the native-born Americans. The reason is very simple. "They know the pit from whence they were digged." Liberty is very sweet to men who have been in a dungeon. It is hunger that makes bread so good to the taste. After the long darkness of oppression, the light of liberty is good to the eyes. Did any of you hear that Italian citizen when he told us why he came to this new land? "Why? Do you ask me, why did I come to your country? Was it that your skies were bluer than Naples? Your cathedrals grander? Your statues more beautiful? Your art more precious? Oh, no! One night, sleeping in my Italian home, I saw a vision and in my dreams, I beheld Liberty, God's dear child, come down to the sands of your seashore. Standing there, she stood with her beautiful face looking eastward toward my land, and stretching out her white arms, she whispered: 'Venite! Venite! Come, come, my dear children.' Obedient to Liberty's command, lo, all these Italians are here." Those of you who heard that apostrophe know that eloquence is not yet dead. Nor can it die so long as these people cherish such unbounded enthusiasm toward the republic that already they call it "My Country."[30]

The civics reader included patriotic boosters at the end of each chapter such as the following:

> The flag of the Republic protects more than 15,000,000 foreign-born persons in the United States and every alien can well join the poet who wrote the following stanzas:
>
> > "Flag of our mighty Union, hail!
> > Blessings abound where thou dost float,

---

[30] Peter Roberts, *English for Coming Americans, Second Reader* (New York: Association Press, 1912), p. 158. See also "Immigrant Blood In National Leaders," pp. 161-62, "What is Patriotism," pp. 177-78, and "What is Americanization," pp. 183-84.

>
> Best robe for Freedom's living form,
> Fit pall to spread upon her tomb,
> Should Heaven to death devote.
>
> "Wave over us in glory still,
> And be our guardian as now,
> Each wind of Heaven salutes thy
>   streaks!
> And withered be the arm that seeks
> To bring that banner low."[31]

The militant patriots considerably influenced not only the Roberts Method, but the entire effort of the Industrial Department toward immigrants. The department distributed a wide variety of literature and pamphlets reminiscent of the cultural onslaught of the N.A.C.L. Some of the titles tell much of their emphasis: "Winners in American Democracy," "Americanization Through Christian Leadership," "Americanization YMCA," and "The Immigrant Guide." This last pamphlet urged the immigrant to "live respectable and clean . . . don't gamble . . . and avoid all persons with unclean lips. . . ." Another repeated the theme of how easily foreigners could rise to the top in America.[32]

The immigrant gatherings put on by the YMCA also reflected the militant nationalism of the N.A.C.L. influence. Whether simple English classes, health clinics, or outdoor celebrations, the immigrant programs were dominated by a sense of patriotism. At an English class in New York City, the entire classroom wall was draped with an American flag. A picture of a "Patriotic Health Talk" put on by the Chicago YMCA, showed a meeting hall filled with young boys surrounded by American flags every thirty feet or so. Another English class was pictured in a large auditorium where the entire stage was draped with a huge American flag, approximately 30 feet by 10 feet. At still another large YMCA hall, several hundred foreign men and women stood before a stage dominated by three huge flags and a giant picture of George Washington. The immigrant attending YMCA rallies or classes could scarcely escape the message that he was expected to worship American heroes and cement American loyalties.[33]

---

[31]Peter Roberts, *Civics for Coming Americans* (New York: Association Press, 1912), p. 17.

[32]"Winners in American Democracy," these and many other pamphlets were found in the Immigration Box.

[33]Pictures and postcards in Immigration Box. See also "Industrial Service, New York City," *The Intercollegian*, XXXII (June, 1910), pp. 254-56.

Whatever differences Roberts might have had with the militant nationalists, all were subsumed with the coming of World War I. The Immigration Department reported that it was "promoting preparedness by helping hundreds of coming Americans to get the Christian idea of Americanism along with their citizenship papers." Roberts himself went to work for the War Work Council under the Education Bureau to help meet "America's military needs." His new task was to convince the immigrants that they should not merely be Americans, but that they should fight. In some army camps, over 200 indoctrination classes were given in order to "help them [the immigrants] to understand why they are in the service and to reconcile them to it." The Industrial Department also went to work for the government as a troubleshooter in labor-management flareups. By 1918, in fact, the Association was sure enough of its reputation that it bargained rather roughly with the government. One committee report asserted, "It is understood that no commitment will be made [to help the government as a labor troubleshooter] until the financial resources are definitely assured."

The YMCA reacted to the war in two ways. First, it redoubled its efforts to Americanize the foreigner.[35] More dramatically, the YMCA organized an intensified propaganda barrage to be used in the army camps. Peter Roberts wrote a new text for use in the cantonment areas. The selections in his indoctrination reader equalled in unabashed chauvinism anything the committee on Public Information ever put out. The chapter headings read like a D.A.R. rally: "Democracy or Despotism--Which?" "The Eyes of the World Are On You," "The Message of the Flag," "The Fourth of July," "The Friends of Freedom," "Our War," "All Classes Respond," "A Mother in Camp." One article, "War on Women," asked the immigrant, "You are not willing to do your bit to stop the Kaiser from murdering women and children?" Incongruously, almost comically interspersed between each selection were instructions to the teacher: "Read the lesson carefully again and let the pupils classify the pronouns in it. . . . Take the second paragraph and let the pupils point out the verbs and state which pass on the action to an object."[36] Roberts never lost sight of his Roberts Method.

The war did not force the YMCA to inaugurate an Americanization program characterized by emotional patriotism. Rather, the militant nationalism which had been an important ingredient in the immigration program from the beginning came to full maturity during the war. The YMCA, despite the best intentions of Peter Roberts and

---

[35]See, for example, the pamphlet "Don't Be A Slacker" (New York: Industrial Department, 1917), which urges YMCA workers to intensify their assault on "the unassimilated foreign element in our population." Immigration Box.

[36]Peter Roberts, *English Reader For Use In Cantonment Areas* (New York: Association Press, 1917), pp. 46-47 and *passim*.

many others, developed a program which was either ineffective, or part of the cultural offensive of much of reform-minded America. As for the card identification system, those who needed it most--foreign-speaking transients--benefited from it least. The in-transit program suffered because the Association agents dared not agitate for better conditions aboard ships. The Ellis Island assistance was evidently quite restricted and did not contact the immigrant until the horror story was over.

The YMCA became a part of the cultural cold war in two ways. First, since the Association was so dependent upon local industry, its industrial educational program became industry's tool. To businessmen, immigrants were employees. Industrialists demanded training in which the careful inculcation of values and habits would transform a largely pre-industrial people into useful and responsive workers in the industrial system. The YMCA program, so far as it was subverted by local industry, became a partner in this attempt at cultural metamorphosis. Second, the YMCA immigration program was profoundly influenced, perhaps "controlled" is not too strong a term, by the militant nationalists who saw the immigrant not as a worker, but as a threat. Unless the immigrant could be transformed into a docile, non-radical, middle class, enthusiastically patriotic American, these cultural cold warriors would not accept him.

For moderates such as Peter Roberts, the state of affairs must have been distressing. How must it have felt to want to be so subtle in the assimilation process and end up working in cantonment camps with the most blatant kind of propaganda? Perhaps Roberts was simply caught up in the blind chauvinism of the war spirit. But one would like to think that as he helped the immigrant soldier find transitive verbs he was choking on the content.

In balance, this analysis of the YMCA may be harsh. Focusing as it does on the limitations of the immigration programs, on the restrictions of business paternalism, and on the influence of the militant patriots, it may not do justice to what the YMCA did accomplish. Thousands of immigrants, after all, did learn rudimentary English through the Roberts method. There is no way to discover how many immigrant lives and limbs were saved in industry by virtue of the worker's ability to react to a warning in time, or to understand instructions properly for new and hazardous machinery. Nor were all of the values and habits undesirable which the cultural assault attempted to inculcate in the foreigners. The method was often harsh and even crude. It was sad that many in the YMCA leadership failed to see the worth and dignity of the immigrants as they were. A few did. Some immigrants, such as the Jewish prodigy who described a YMCA Americanization class as "humiliating tripe" reacted indignantly to the more strident aspects of the YMCA programs. But probably the vast majority of the common immigrants agreed with the appreciation expressed by the following immigrant adult in a letter to his YMCA teacher:

My Dir School [teacher]:

    I am wraiting letter. I am student.
I laik thet naith [night] school wery moch.
I keep the wery strong a[nd] wont [want]
work wery hart a biciem [and become] wais
[wise] boy. Letter to thicher.[37]
                                  Felix

    In the final analysis, the YMCA program probably did the immigrant no grievous harm. Sadly enough though, its inherent restrictions and co-optations prevented its accomplishing so much more.

---

[37] Norbert Wiener, *Ex-Prodigy: My Childhood and Youth* (New York: Simon and Schuster, 1953), pp. 266-67. Letter from Felix contained in pamphlet published by the Chicago YMCA (1911), Immigration Box. Several interesting immigrant letters of petition for night school English classes are reprinted in "Night Schools for Americanizing Immigrants," *The Immigrants in America Review*, II (April, 1916), pp. 35-37. Five fascinating letters from Polish immigrants concerning many aspects of their life in America are in W. I. Thomas, "Five Polish Peasant Letters," *ibid.*, pp. 58-63.

EPILOGUE

REFLECTIONS ON THOREAU AND CULTURAL PLURALISM

"Give me your tired, your poor, your
huddled masses yearning to breathe
free. . . ."
    Statue of Liberty

"If a man does not keep pace with
his companions, perhaps it is because he hears a different drummer.
Let him step to the music which he
hears - however measured or far
away."
    Thoreau

"The crucible does not do its work
unless it turns out those cast into
it in one national mold and that
must be the mold established by
Washington and his fellows when they
made us into a nation."[1]
    Theodore Roosevelt

  The historian has neatly compartmentalized the progressive era. He has written of corrupt political machines, greedy industrial tycoons, crusading muckrakers, backward immigrants, frightened nativists, kind-hearted settlement and charity workers, persistent labor organizers, and rejected radicals. If inclined toward revisionism, the historian has painfully, even shockingly, rearranged the adjectives. In either case, he has portrayed the actors in the progressive drama as so many organizations and pressure groups interacting with and against each other, all the while themselves being molded by the inexorable forces of industrialism and urbanization.

  If historians have dwelled on the pressure groups of the progressive era, it has been in an effort to reflect reality.

---

[1] From "Children of the Crucible," in Cushing Strout, *The American Image of the Old World* (New York: Harper Row, 1963), p. 150.

Certainly, the period was characterized by an astounding growth of organizations. Patriotic geneological societies, immigration restrictionist groups, settlement houses, professional associations, the new version of the Ku Klux Klan--even the Boy Scouts--began during or immediately preceding the progressive years. Each organization attempted to combat that evil which it thought most threatening. Yet in keeping with the adage "you become what you hate," the progressives tended to imitate the evil they opposed in direct proportion to the intensity of their fear of it.

The groups examined in this study were unified by a common fear of cultural inundation. Charity workers were afraid that the American city would deteriorate under the influence of the swarms of foreign paupers. Settlement organizers feared that their customs and traditions were slowly surrendering to the forces of cosmopolitanism. The educators saw themselves as beleaguered defenders of the cultural integrity of the native Anglo-Saxon stock. The YMCA, dominated as it was by local industry and the North American Civic League, insisted that education must bring about cultural and political conformity.

Because these organizations feared the cultural offensive of the aliens, they launched a cultural offensive of their own. Likewise, they feared that American institutions were becoming the exclusive domain of the boss and his foreign machine. In proportion to the intensity of that fear, they attempted to preserve their nation as the exclusive domain of those who thought and acted as they did. Thus, they established a machine of their own. They approached American society just as East Side House approached the Monday night dance. Only those of the proper decorum could enter.

Perhaps the most unfortunate part of the cultural cold war was its lack of necessity. Immigrants certainly posed no unified threat to existing American values. They exhibited to the utmost of human endurance their willingness to work hard and save money. Their children so quickly accepted American values that they caused severe strains on old world traditions. Immigrants established all kinds of self-help organizations so as to avoid American charity--the immigrant bank, press, neighborhood store, church, ward healer, close family structure and labor contractor to name a few. But all of these efforts also helped to keep intact the immigrants' sense of cultural identity. To the American cultural cold warriors, then, immigrant institutions were a threat in proportion to their effectiveness.

This is not to say that immigrants or their institutions were faultless. Indeed, the immigrants brought with them their prejudices. Their institutions, including the political boss, were often patronizing and exploitive. But the cold warriors condemned the immigrant not because he was prejudiced, but because he did not share their prejudice. They condemned the boss not because he was exploitive, but because he represented an effective defense against their cultural offensive. They condemned the other self-help organizations not because they did not work, but because they did.

The lot of the immigrant might have been worse had it not been for the settlements, charities, educators and the YMCA's. But, as likely, the immigrant might have done quite well relying on his own frugality, industry, and ingenuity. He might have preserved much more of his cultural heritage and still have been able to advance into America's economic mainstream. After all, beyond a knowledge of the English language, there was little necessary to survive and prosper in America that the immigrant did not already have. Certainly he wanted to succeed on his own, but the cultural cold warriors would not let him.

Of the three quotations which introduce this epilogue, clearly Theodore Roosevelt spoke for his era. By the time of his presidency, the inscription on the Statue of Liberty represented a rapidly vanishing point of view. But the strangest idea of all, particularly to the progressive cold warriors, was that each man must be allowed to follow his own drummer. To a generation searching desperately for cultural conformity, Henry Thoreau's words must have sounded threatening indeed. The progressive impulse to organize, organize, organize was a manifestation of the decline of the individual in the rapidly emerging corporate, industrial state. For in direct proportion as a man became a cog in an organization, so did he lose regard for the individual and become less an individual himself. The immigrants had the misfortune of trying to step to a different cultural drummer at a time when Thoreau was long dead and forgotten.

APPENDIX A-1

CONTRACT BETWEEN THE BOY AND HIS EMPLOYER

FITCHBURG INDUSTRIAL SCHOOL

Rules and Conditions

Under Which Special Apprentices Taking the Four-Year Co-operative Industrial Course at the High School of Fitchburg are Received for Instruction at the Works of
----

First. The applicant for apprenticeship under this agreement must have satisfactorily met requirements for entrance to this course at the high school.

Second. The apprentice is to work for us continuously, well and faithfully, under such rules and regulations as may prevail at the works of the above company, for the term of approximately 4,950 hours, commencing with the acceptance of this agreement, in such capacity and on such work as specified below.

LATHE WORK.
PLANER WORK.
DRILLING.
BENCH AND FLOOR WORK.
AND SUCH OTHER MACHINE WORK, ACCORDING TO THE CAPABILITY OF THE APPRENTICE, AS PERTAINS TO OUR BRANCH OF MANUFACTURING.

This arrangement of work to be binding unless changed by mutual agreement of all parties to this contract.

Third. The apprentice shall report to his employer for work every alternate week when the high school is in session and on all working-days when the high school is not in session, except during vaction periods provided below, and he shall be paid only for actual time at such work.

Fourth. The apprentice is to have a vacation, without pay, of two weeks each year during school vacation.

Fifth. The employer reserves the right to suspend regular work wholly, or in part, at any time it may be deemed necessary, and agrees to provide under ordinary conditions other work at the regular rate of pay for the apprentice during such period.

Sixth. Should the conduct or work of the apprentice not be satisfactory to employer or to the high-school authority, he may at any time be dismissed or suspended for a time by the employer, without previous notice. The first two months of the apprentice's shop-work are considered a trial time.

Seventh. Lost time shall be made up before the expiration of each year, at the rate of wages paid during said year, and no year of service shall commence till after all lost time by the apprentice in the preceding year shall have been fully made up.

Eighth. The apprentice must purchase from time to time such tools as may be required for doing rapid and accurate work.

Ninth. The said term of approximately 4,950 hours (three-year shop term) shall be divided into three periods as stated below, and the compensation shall be as follows, payable on regular pay days to each apprentice:

For the first period of approximately 1,650 hours----------10 cents per hour.

For the second period of approximately 1,650 hours---------11 cents per hour.

For the third period of approximately 1,650 hours----------12-1/2 cents per hour.

Tenth. The above wage scale shall begin the first day of July preceding the apprentice's entrance upon the first year of shopwork of the high school industrial course.

These papers, subject to the two months' trial noted in paragraph 6, shall be signed by the two parties to the contract at the time the boy enters the shop.

The satisfactory fulfillment of the conditions of this contract leads to a diploma, to be conferred upon the apprentice by the school board of Fitchburg upon his graduation, which diploma shall bear the signature of an officer of the company with which he served his apprenticeship.

APPENDIX A-2

AGREEMENT BETWEEN PARTIES

THIS AGREEMENT made the _____ day of _____ A.D., 191_, by and between _____ of _____ party of the
(Employer)
first part, and _____ of _____ party of the second
(Apprentice)
part.

    Witnesseth, That the party of the second part shall from the date hereof, for the term of three years (4,950 hours divided into three periods of 1,650 hours a year, as stated in the "Rules and conditions"), and so much longer as may be necessary to make up lost time, become and be the apprentice of the party of the first part to the art or trade of _____ and that said parties of the first and second parts will well and truly do and perform all things required to be done and performed by them in and by said rules and conditions of the cooperative industrial course.

    In witness whereof said party of the first part has caused these presents to be signed and sealed by _____ its _____ for this purpose authorized, and said party of the second part has hereto set his hand and seal this day and year first above written.

    Signed and sealed _____
                        (Employer)

In presence of _____

    Signed and sealed _____
                        (Apprentice)

In presence of _____

APPENDIX A-3

AGREEMENT OF RELATIVE OR GUARDIAN

I _____ of the above named _____
(Apprentice)
do hereby give my consent to his entering the employ of the said

_____ upon the terms named in the above articles of agree-
(Employer)
ment; and I further agree that in consideration of such employment

the wages or earnings of my said _____ shall be paid
(Son or ward)
directly to him, and I hereby release all claim that I now have or

may have hereafter thereto.

    Dated at _____ this ____ day of _____ 191__.

    Signed and sealed _____
                            (Relative or guardian)

In presence of _____

_____

    This is to certify that the within named _____
Completed his term of apprenticeship.

                                                     _____(Seal)

APPENDIX A-4

PRACTICAL SUGGESTIONS

Each boy when he enters shop work is presented with the following suggestions:

CO-OP INFORMATION

Read this carefully. It will save you and us trouble.

Remember that the object of work is production. Your foreman measures you by the quantity and quality of your work. Social position does not enter. In the shop you are not a high school boy; you are an apprentice. Wear clothes accordingly. If you get the mistaken idea that any work given you is beneath the dignity of a high school boy, just remember you are an apprentice and get 100 per cent busy.

It is your business to get along smoothly with the workmen and foreman; not theirs to get along with you.

Do not expect any personal attention from the superintendent. He will probably ignore you entirely, but he knows whether or not you are making good, and in most cases his idea of you depends upon your ability to please your foreman.

Don't be a kicker and don't continually bother your foreman for higher wages. If you are not receiving your raises as agreed upon, or if you have other grievances, let the director adjust matters through the firm's office.

An idle machine means a cash loss to the firm. Let yours never be idle without previous arrangement. To "lay off" without permission is a serious offense for a workingman and is just as serious for an apprentice, regardless of the relative importance of the work he does.

The foreman always plans ahead for every man's work, yours included. Therefore, notify your foreman before you leave on any regular vacation. A little thoughtfulness may prevent serious misunderstanding. And always, if sick and unable to report in person, send a telephone message to your foreman. He can arrange then to have your work done for you; otherwise he will naturally cease to depend on you.

Never try to conceal defective work. Take your full measure of blame, and do not make the same mistake twice.

Watch, in a quiet way, what things are being done around you, and don't be afraid to ask sensible questions. A good rule is to think over a question twice before asking. A reputation for having "horse sense" means that you are making good.

Foreman and workmen will take pleasure in showing you, if you show yourself genuinely appreciative of little attentions. If they tell you something you already know, don't spoil their pleasure by telling them you already know it, but let it be impressed on your mind all the deeper; for the conversation may lead to something which is entirely new to you.

If your foreman refuses to grant any requests, and you value his good will, do not refer the matter to a higher official. Let the director, Mr. Hunter, help you.

The fool act of one co-op hurts every co-op. See that your actions in and out of the shop do not bring discredit on the co-op course.

Confer freely with Mr. Hunter about your work. He is here to help you do the right thing and be a <u>success</u>.

APPENDIX A-5

Collateral reading (for English course for all those entered in co-op plan--Fitchburg High School) is required from books on trades, such as the following:

Young Folks' Library of Vocations. Boston Hall & Locke Co.

Vocation for Girls. Houghton & Mifflin Co.

Bulletins of Vocation Bureau of Boston.

Harper's Electricity Book for Boys. Adams.

Harper's Machinery Book for Boys. Adams.

Boys' Book of Inventions. Baker.

Boys' Second Book of Inventions. Baker.

History of the Telephone. Casson.

Romance of Industry and Invention. Cochrane.

Romance of Modern Electricity. Gibson.

Romance of Modern Manufacture. Gibson.

Life Stories of Undistinguished Americans. Holt.

Triumphs of Science. Lane.

Careers of Danger and Daring. Moffat.

Hand work in Wood. Noyes.

Harper's How to Understand Electrical Work. Onken & Baker.

Artist's Way of Working in the Various Handicrafts and Arts of Design. Two vols. Sturgis.

Story of the Railroad. Warman.

Romance of Modern Engineering. Williams.

Romance of Modern Invention. Williams.

Romance of Modern Mechanism. Williams.

Romance of Modern Steam Locomotion. Williams.

The Workers. Two vols. Syckoff.

APPENDIX B-1

ROBERTS METHOD ENGLISH INDUSTRIAL SERIES

CARD PRACTICE ON LESSONS 1 and 2
    (Industrial Series)

1. Where are you working?
2. I work in the cotton mill.
3. Do you take the car in going to work?
4. No, I walk to work in the morning.
5. Do you take the car when you go home?
6. Yes, sometimes.
7. Does the trolley car pass the gate of the mill?
8. No, the street car line is two blocks away.
9. How far have you to walk to the shop?
10. From the house it is ten minutes' walk.
11. How far from the gate of the mill?
12. It is only a few minutes' walk.
13. Where do you keep your tools?
14. I keep them in a box.
15. Please tell me how you begin the day's work.
16. I enter the mill and take off my hat and coat. I put these on the nail near by.
17. I then roll up my sleeves and I begin the work of the day.
18. Does the foreman come to you?
19. Yes, he passes me as he goes through the mill.
20. Are you able to talk to him?
21. Yes, if he takes time to talk.
22. Is the foreman kind to you?
23. Yes, if I do what he tells me.
24. Do you always do what he tells you?
25. Yes, I try to, but sometimes I don't understand.

CARD PRACTICE ON LESSONS 3 and 4
    (Industrial Series)

1. Did you shine your shoes this morning?
2. Yes, I went to the shoe stand and got a polish.
3. Did he give you a good shine?
4. Yes, he took care to put on a fine gloss, and he blackened the rim of the sole.
5. Did he brush your clothes also?
6. Yes, when I got off the chair, he took the whisk and brushed my clothes.
7. Do you generally go there for a shine?
8. Yes, I know the boy, and am interested in him.
9. Are you interested in miners?
10. Yes, I know some men who work in the mines.

APPENDIX B-1 (continued)

11. Have you seen them going to work?
12. Yes, some of them go down shafts, some go down slopes, and some enter drifts.
13. Have you seen them at work?
14. Yes, I have visited coal mines and been in some chambers.
15. How did they appear to you?
16. They had no coat and vest on and the sleeves of their shirt were tucked up.
17. Were they black?
18. Yes, the coal dust blackens them.
19. Are they hard workers?
20. Yes, the miners work hard.

CARD PRACTICE ON LESSONS 5 and 6
(Industrial Series)

1. Where are you working?
2. I work on the railroad in summer and work in the steel mill in winter.
3. What do you do on the railroad?
4. I dig and shovel dirt and carry sleepers and rails.
5. What tools do you use?
6. I use the pick and shovel, the steel bar and sledge hammer.
7. Do you work in the same place?
8. No, the gang goes from place to place to fix the track.
9. How do you like the work?
10. All right, if it is not too hot in summer.
11. Why do you go to the steel mill?
12. Because it is too cold in winter to work on the railroad.
13. What do you do in the steel mill?
14. Laboring work. I carry scrap iron to the wagon and clean around the mill.
15. What tools do you use in the mill?
16. Mostly the shovel, but sometimes the pick and the sledge hammer.
17. Do you go from place to place in the mill?
18. Yes, the foreman leads us where there is work to be done.
19. Is the work hard?
20. Sometimes when we carry heavy iron scrap.

APPENDIX B-1 (continued)

CARD PRACTICE ON LESSONS 7 and 8
    (Industrial Series)

1. Are you out of work, John?
2. Yes, I quit my job yesterday.
3. Why did you give up your work?
4. Because it was too hard for me.
5. Did they pay you pretty well?
6. No, the wages were not what they ought to be.
7. What other objection did you have to the job?
8. I worked in a very hot place and I could not stand it any longer.
9. What are you going to do now?
10. I'm going to look for another job.
11. Where are you going?
12. I expect to go down to the mill to-morrow and see the foreman.
13. I have a friend in the mill, would you like an introduction to him?
14. Yes, I would; I shall be thankful for any help you can give me.
15. What time do you expect to go to the mill in the morning?
16. I will go down at seven o'clock.
17. Will you meet me at the gate of the mill?
18. Yes, I shall be very glad to do so.
19. Would you wish me to say a kind word for you to the foreman?
20. Indeed I would, for I am anxious to get work.
21. Have you any money?
22. Yes, a few dollars, but they will soon go with a family to keep.
23. Well, meet me to-morrow at the gate of the mill, good-bye.

CARD PRACTICE ON LESSONS 9 and 10
    (Industrial Series)

1. Did you hear about Jim?
2. No, what is the matter?
3. Jim was injured this morning in the work.
4. Do you know how it happened?
5. Yes, I was near him when he was hurt.
6. Tell me how it happened.
7. Jim was hitching the chain to a piece of casting. When the crane raised the casting,
8. the chain slipped and down came the iron upon Jim's foot.
9. Was he hurt very badly?

APPENDIX B-1 (continued)

10. Yes, his foot was badly bruised.
11. Did the doctor dress his foot?
12. Yes, we tore off his shoe and stocking and the doctor bathed it well,
13. then applied some remedies, and then bandaged it.
14. Where is he now?
15. At home, resting in bed.
16. How does his wife feel?
17. Pretty badly, but she said: "I'm thankful it is not worse."
18. How many children has Jim?
19. He has five, three boys and two girls.
20. They are all small, are they not?
21. Yes, one of the boys began to work lately.
22. We must call and cheer Jim up a little.
23. Yes, the outlook is blue unless some of his friends help him.

APPENDIX B-2

ROBERTS METHOD ENGLISH--COMMERCIAL SERIES

SERIES C--LESSONS 1 and 2

A. Have you written your letter?
B. Yes, I wrote a long letter to my father in homeland.
C. With what did you write--was it a pen or pencil?
D. I wrote with a pen and used blue ink.
E. What did you do when you finished the letter?
F. I folded the paper carefully and put it in the envelope; then I sealed the envelope, put a postage stamp upon it and mailed the letter.
G. Where did you mail the letter?
H. I put it in the letter box on the street corner.
I. Did you then go down town?
J. No. I returned to the house and stayed at home that evening.
K. Do you know where the post office is?
L. Yes. It is located two blocks away.
M. Have you been in the post office?
N. Yes. I was there this morning.
O. Did you buy any stamps there?
P. Yes. I bought five two-cent stamps
Q. Who waited on you?
R. The clerk. He was a short, light-haired, young man.
S. How did you find the place where stamps were sold?
T. I looked for the window above which was the word, "Stamps."
U. Did he give you the right change?
V. Yes. I gave him twenty-five cents. He gave me five two-cent stamps and fifteen cents in cash.
W. Did you use some of the stamps?
X. Yes. I cut them apart, moistened them and put them on the envelopes.
Y. What did you do with the letters?
Z. I saw a slot over which was the word "Letters." I dropped them into that.

APPENDIX B-2 (continued)

SERIES C--LESSONS 3 and 4

A. Are you going away by train?
B. Yes. I expect to take the train to New York City.
C. How are you going to the depot?
D. I will take the street car which passes the depot.
E. Do you know your way?
F. Yes. I asked a policeman two weeks ago, and he kindly directed me.
G. Did you have any difficulty in getting your ticket?
H. No. I saw the window where tickets were sold and I went there and got my ticket.
I. Tell me what the ticket agent did.
J. He took a ticket from the ticket rack, then stamped the date on it, then said, "Two dollars" and placed the ticket on the window counter.
K. Did you have long to wait in the depot?
L. No. The train soon came into the station and I went out to the platform.
M. Do you have any baggage?
N. Yes. I have a trunk which an expressman will bring to the depot.
O. What do you do with the trunk?
P. The expressman leaves it in the baggage room. I go there to identify it and ask the baggage man to check it.
Q. How does he do this?
R. He asks me for my ticket. He punches it. He then takes a check from a hook, attached it to the trunk, and then gives me a brass piece, called a check.
S. What is the check for?
T. It is a receipt to me for my trunk. I keep it carefully, and when I get to New York I go for my trunk.
U. Tell me how you get your trunk.
V. I go to the baggage room, present to the baggage master my check. He goes in search of the trunk. When he finds it, he hands it over to me.
W. How do you get the trunk to the hotel?
X. I ask an employee of a transfer company to have the trunk sent to my hotel.
Y. Do you go with the trunk?
Z. No. The man gives me a card-board check. I go to my hotel and the trunk comes after me.

APPENDIX B-2 (continued)

SERIES C--LESSONS 5 and 6

A. John, can you tell me when is pay-day?
B. Yes, it is the day after to-morrow. That will be Saturday.
C. Do you expect a good pay?
D. Fair. I worked a full week, but no overtime.
E. I expect a poor pay for I lost two days.
F. What happened to you--did you celebrate?
G. No. I was sick. How much do you make per day?
H. Sixteen and a half cents an hour or a dollar sixty-five a day.
I. Is your pay generally correct?
J. Yes. There have been errors once or twice in my pay.
K. Did the boss make it right?
L. Yes. Of course, I had to get after him and show him the error.
M. I find it difficult to make both ends meet, sometimes.
N. Well, that is the case with me also. It is expensive to run a house.
O. What rent do you pay?
P. I pay a dollar a room. We have three rooms which is $12.00 a month.
Q. I find that everything is dear and the money goes quickly.
R. Yes indeed. My bill for butter and eggs, milk and meat, amounts each week to between $3.50 and $4.00.
S. In the winter time my bill for coal runs high.
T. So is mine, and the way coal has advanced in late years is astonishing.
U. That's so, but we must get it, for there is nothing more unpleasant than a cold house.
V. Have you any lodges?
W. Yes, I have two lodges to which I pay, on an average, twenty-five cents a week.
X. Then you have your church to pay, too. I give to my church, fifty cents a month.
Y. My church dues are more than that. It costs me each week, 25c., when all items are added up.
Z. Well, it could be worse. As long as I can work we can get along, but should sickness come, then it is a pinch.

APPENDIX B-2 (continued)

SERIES C--LESSONS 7, 8 and 9

A. You have bought a new suit of clothes?
B. Yes. I bought this suit yesterday. How do you like it?
C. It fits you very well indeed, and I think the goods in it is all right.
D. Thank you. I hope it will be a serviceable suit.
E. Are you going to make a trip to fatherland in that new suit?
F. No. I don't expect to go there this year, but I have sent a present there.
G. What do you mean?
H. I sent some money to my folks last week.
I. Tell me, please, how you sent the money.
J. I went to the post office, filled out a foreign order blank, then put it in the hand of the money-order clerk.
K. And what did he give you?
L. He gave me a post-office order which I enclosed in the envelope and sent to fatherland.
M. Did the clerk give you a receipt?
N. Yes. I kept it for some time and then destroyed it when I heard from the folks that they had cashed the order.
O. It must have been pleasant for them to get the cash.
P. Yes. They thanked me very much. I like to remember the folks at home.
Q. How do you keep your spare cash?
R. I have opened an account in the savings bank of town.
S. Tell me how to do this.
T. You go to the bank, tell the cashier you want to open an account and he will accommodate you.
U. Have you anthing to pay?
V. No. All you have to do is to sign your name and take the bank book the cashier gives you.
W. What is the bank book for?
X. Every time you deposit money, the sum is entered on this book, so that you may see what account you have in the bank.
Y. Does the bank pay any interest on the money?
Z. Yes. Three per cent is paid in the bank in which I have an account. I think the bank is the safest way to keep spare cash until we get the postal savings bank.
A.1 What is a postal savings bank?
A.2 It is a provision made by the Government to receive the spare cash of working men in the post office where we now get our stamps.
A.3 And will the Government keep the money safely?
A.4 It will be as safe as the credit of the Government, and back of the Government are the people of the United States.

AYPENDIX B-2 (continued)

SERIES C--LESSONS 10 and 11

A. Michael, I heard you had bought a lot?
B. Yes. I bought a lot on Sherman St. in the fifth ward.
C. What did you pay for it?
D. The owner asked $400. I offered him $350 and got the lot.
E. In transferring the property, what was necessary?
F. I secured a lawyer to look up the title in order to
    see that the property had no encumbrances.
G. What was then necessary?
H. When the deed was delivered to me, I took it to the
    Court House to have it properly registered.
I. What is the process of registering a deed?
J. You take it to the clerk in the office of Register
    of Deeds, leave it with him for a week or ten
    days and then call for it again.
K. You pay something, I suppose.
L. Yes. The cost of registering a deed is generally
    between $2.50 and $3.00.
M. Are you going to build a house on the lot?
N. Yes, that is my intention.
O. How do you proceed in the matter of building a
    house?
P. I first find out what kind of house I need, then ask
    some contractor to bid upon the plans.
Q. Do you give the contract to the lowest bidder?
R. That depends upon the man. The cheapest man
    is not always the safest.
S. How must the contractor proceed?
T. He must get a building permit from the proper
    authority before he can proceed.
U. How do you make your payments?
V. According as the work proceeds.
W. Will you move into the house when it is finished?
X. Yes, I hope to. Of course, the house must be
    dry before I move into it.
Y. How long will it take to dry the house?
Z. It partly depends on the weather and the amount
    of fire put in the house.

APPENDIX B-3

NORTH AMERICAN CIVIC LEAGUE FOR IMMIGRANTS
*Messages for New Comers to the
United States*
(Boston: N.A.C.L., n.d.)

MESSAGE THREE

THE STORY OF THE AMERICAN PEOPLE

<u>HISTORY</u>

It is good to have a country. A great Bostonian has written a story about a man who had none. He was very miserable and unhappy. There was no flag for him to cheer; no place for him to call home. Every one who reads that tale and who has and loves a country, feels his heart thrill. Some to whom this word comes were born across the water and do not expect to become Americans. Very well--be true then to the country of your birth and cherish it, your homeland. Others think of this land as their country or expect to make it their country as soon as they can comply with the naturalization laws. It is right for such to think tenderly of their birthplace, but it is also right to seek by every means to show their love for the United States because they have decided to cast in their fortunes with its people.

There is no better way to indicate this than to obey its laws. When children love their parents they are prompt to obey. It is the same with patriots--they delight to comply with the ordinances of the city in which they reside, and the laws of the state and nation. But the country expects more of a citizen than obedience. It requires loyalty and devotion. It has a right to ask that a citizen shall not only do what is required of him, but shall help support its institutions by paying a tax proportionate to his property, and in case of war or breach of the peace, shall offer his services. It has also a right to expect from a citizen an intelligent interest in its affairs and a pride in its accomplishments.

In America it is sure of the former because every one has a hand in managing the affairs of the State, and it is sure of the latter provided people are kept informed of the great deeds of former generations.

Since it is desirable to nourish the sort of national pride that is wholesome and leads to noble endeavor, the country depends upon citizens who were born beneath the stars and stripes (the American flag) to tell their children of its past glories, but it is no less concerned that new citizens should hear its story. To accomplish such a purpose is the object of this message.

It may be known to some of you that when the first settlers came to North America they found nothing but vast forests which sheltered wild men and beasts. It was a savage wilderness. So inhospitable to those who did not understand how to meet its conditions, that at first, progress in clearing the woods and developing its riches was very slow. So tedious in fact that only a hundred years ago the greater part of the country was uninhabited.

Then with the establishment of a government that guaranteed independence and opportunity for all who were willing to work conscientiously, a great movement started toward the West which attracted many of the bravest hearts in Europe, as well as in the cities by the shore. The result has been as wonderful as a fairy tale. Some of the accomplishments being so recent that men still in middle life remember when lands now producing great crops of corn and wheat were spoken of as deserts.

This is the country that you have come to, and of which many of you will become citizens. More than eighty millions of people are occupying it now, and there are few sections which have not been visited, although there is hardly any part of the land which is not capable of supporting many more men, women and children than at present live in it.

If you remember what was said in the opening about the conditions of the land two hundred years ago, you will understand why scholars agree that never in the world's history has there been such a wonderful growth. You will also understand how desirable it is to be industrious, frugal, honest and brave, for it is plainly owing to the fact that the pioneers and their followers and descendants have possessed all these virtues that the winning of the wilderness was made possible.

The first settlements, as you know, were made by Englishmen, some in the north about Boston, some in the south as at Jamestown and in Maryland, and some in Pennsylvania. There were Dutchmen in New York and Spaniards and Frenchmen in other parts of North America, but the most enterprising settlers were the English, and the most successful of their colonies were those in which the people were high minded and liberty loving.

A great ocean separated these people from the king to whom they had originally owed allegiance, and it is not surprising that he did not bother himself to think much about their needs. The king knew that they were poor, and that they would have a hard time fighting the savages if they wished to protect their homes and whatever property they might acquire. He thought of them as more likely to prove a burden than a source of wealth, and so he left them to take care of their own affairs. It was a fortunate happening. Left to themselves without anything to weaken them, but with every condition favorable to develop virtue, they quickly found two things to be true,--first, that liberty was sweeter than life,--second, that liberty could not be maintained without order. To secure the latter they all agreed to abide by certain rules to be made and enforced by men chosen by the majority of the citizens. Thus they laid the foundations of free government, and drew to themselves new recruits from men oppressed by tyranny in the older countries of the world.

Meanwhile they were acquiring wealth--for wars with the savages and the hard work required to fell the great trees and drive the plough through the new land had made the men fearless and valiant, the women patient and uncomplaining. Framing the laws to meet their requirements, and bringing up their children to be virtuous and self-reliant, it is not surprising that they were soon able to supply all their wants and to put away something for a rainy day. Then the king, who had almost forgotten them, woke up and commenced to meddle in their affairs. This they did not like. As a consequence contests between the king's ministers and the colonists followed one another, until one day the monarch resolved to tax the Americans, without permitting them to have anything to say about it. This was a serious mistake. Grown accustomed to manage their own affairs, the colonists refused to submit to such interference. They took up arms and first at Lexington and Bunker Hill near Boston, and then in many other places met the king's soldiers in battle. There were defeats and victories as in all wars, but the result was as might have been expected. The Americans won their freedom! This was more than a hundred years ago. So dearly did the people prize their liberties which they had fought so bravely to maintain, that before establishing a government they sent their wisest men into conference to prepare a constitution (a written paper stating just how they would govern themselves).--

There were those who did not wish to have such a compact, because they felt it would prove a restraint when conditions changed. But the men who knew how hateful tyranny was and who had suffered so much by reason of it, were fearful that their children's children would forget how easily they might bring back the old conditions and would do something foolish that would enslave them. Therefore a constitution was drawn up and made the supreme law of the land to be changed only by vote of the whole people.

Under its provisions the United States has prospered beyond the dream of those who framed it. During the benign administration of George Washington, who had led the armies of the colonists in the great war in which they had been victorious, and which is spoken of as the Revolution, the new country won a place among the nations. It was a great period! Washington was extolled by the wise and virtuous everywhere for his bravery and his moderation, and the new constitution was read by patriots in many distant lands. As a result a tide of immigration set in toward the ports of the United States, bringing millions of the best people to cast in their lot with the Americans and enjoy the privileges of a free country.

That these new-comers were welcome you all know. You also know something of the way in which the people, overcoming great obstacles, pushed their villages westward until they reached first the Rocky Mountains and then the Pacific Ocean which separates America from the Orient.

You can easily understand how it followed soon afterwards that men living hundreds of miles apart and under different conditions, those in one section working in factories, and those in another region tilling the soil, should have commenced to feel independent of each other. You can also understand how reading the Constitution differently, these same men quarrelled, with the result that the country would have been split in twain by the great conflict that ensued, had not the real feeling of the whole people that progress and liberty could only be secured by union, triumphed. This war which threatened the destruction of the United States was one of the severest in the world's history; men on either side performed prodigies of valor and won the admiration of Europe. But after it was over and the wise conviction of the majority that union was necessary had prevailed, the people of different sections were drawn together by closer ties than ever before and the Constitution became a sacred document.

The greatest American during the war which is known as the War of the Secession, was Abraham Lincoln, the president, who had been a poor boy and knew the heart of the people. By every talent he possessed he sought to keep his countrymen in close alliance in order that--to quote his own words--"a government of the people, for the people and by the people shall not perish from the earth."

Americans hold no name in greater reverence than that of Abraham Lincoln.

If you are to become an American citizen, you will play a part in the next era. The United States possesses marvelous wealth and has a great history. It is believed that the character of its citizens will be strengthened by intermarriage with the sturdy people of other races, and that its future is assured.

APPENDIX B-4

ELLIS ISLAND PROCESSING

REPORT OF E. S. TOWSON
YMCA Representative, 1907

The Incoming Ship

Every ship is brought into port by a United States pilot. A message is sent from the incoming ship to Sandy Hook, giving the number of passengers of each class carried. The mail is taken off and the ship proceeds to quarantine. There it is examined by the New York Health Officers.

New York is the only port of entry where quarantine is not under control of the United States government.

The Medical Staffs at all immigrant Stations are of course under the general Government, being a detail of the Public Health & Marine Service Department of the Treasury.

The ship being inspected at quarantine is now met by the United States Custom Officers and then by representatives of the Boarding Division of the Department of Immigration; this consists of Immigration Inspectors, Doctor and Boarding Matrons.

The Boarding Division

The office of the Boarding Division is not at Ellis Island, but at the Barge Office, Battery.

Through the courtesy of Commissioner Watshorn I accompanied the boarding party on the tug "Immigration" six miles down the bay to meet the S.S. "Compania."

Beside this great ship, by no means among the larger class, down whose smoke stacks a train of cars could go comfortably; our tug seemed a mere toy. From the top deck of the tug we crawled over an ordinary ladder thrown across to the second deck of the steamer.

The Doctors having finished, the Immigration and Custom Officers took charge. One Immigration officer in the First Cabin Dining Room, another in the Second Cabin Dining Room.

The passengers then presented themselves singly and answered such questions as the Immigration officer asked them. The officers had before them copies of the ship's manifest containing history of each passenger. A glance at the manifest, together with long experience told the officer what and how many questions to ask.

The manifest alien passengers contained the following twenty-nine questions any one or all are proper subjects of enquiry for the Immigration officers.

1. Full name.
2. Family name.
3. Age in years and months.
4. Sex.
5. Married or single.
6. Calling or occupation.
7. Able to (a) read (b) Write.
8. Nationality (Country of which citizen is subject).
9. Race or people.
10. Last permanent residence, Country, City or Town.
11. The name and complete address of nearest relative or friend in Country when alien came.
12. Final destination, State, City or Town.
13. Number on list.
14. Whether having ticket to such final destination.
15. By whom was passage paid, whether alien paid his own passage; whether paid by any other person or by any Corporation, Society, Municipality, or Government.
16. Whether in possession of $50, if less how much.
17. Whether if ever before in U.S. and if so where. yes or no. If Yes, year or period of year, where and whom.
18. Whether going to join relative or friend; and if so, what relative or friend, and his name and complete address.
19. Ever in prison or almshouse or institution for care and treatment of Insane, or supported by charity. If so which.
20. Whether a Polygamist.
21. Whether an Anarchist.
22. Whether coming by reason of any offer, solicitation, promise or agreement expressed or implied to labor in the United States.
23. Condition of health, medical and physical.
24. Deformed or crippled, length of time and cause.
25. Height, feet inches.
26. Complexion.
27. Color of hair - eyes.
28. Marks of identification.
29. Place of birth - Country - City or Town.

Questions are not always presented in form given here, but going to the mark, for instance the instant and casual query of the Immigration officer of "Work here" covered the formidable question 22, which decided whether or not the alien was a contract laborer.

The questioning in the 1st. cabin while thorough, was of necessity, more perfunctory than that of the second cabin. In this way were sorted out those to be further examined on board or to be detained at Ellis Island. No matter what the financial or social standing or class, the passenger, if detained, goes to Ellis Island.

After being passed by Immigration Officer all the first and second class passengers declare their baggage to Custom Officers in the first cabin.

For the protection of females none are allowed to leave the ship except under supervision of bonafide relative or friends or a matron of the Travellers Aid Society.

Boarding Matrons and Travellers Aid Society

The duties of the Boarding Matrons are to pick our [sic] prostitutes (17 of these women were spotted and deported last year). To protect those females landing in New York and to assist others passing through to Railroad Stations. Example, a young lady, an alien, destination Philadelphia, having ticket there, was detained in the dining room until her uncle was found on the dock by a Boarding Matron and girl was delivered to him. Had the uncle failed to meet her, she would have been turned over to a matron of the Travellers Aid Society, who meets every ship, taken by her to Jersey City, and if long wait, put in charge of Station matron of the Travellers Aid Society whose care is absolute as if she were a United States officer.

This society is supported by wealthy women of New York City, Travellers Aid Matrons live in a house for that purpose on 48th Street. The society has a shelter for respectable girls at 212 E. 46th Street under care of Sister Eleanor of the Eposcipal [sic] Church.

I saw among many others detained for other reasons a highly intelligent and respectable English woman of 55, having with her $300, intending to visit sisters at points in Louisiana and Miss. All right in every way, was held for assistance and care.

Y.M.C.A. might do work for young men similar, if not identical with that done by Travellers Aid Society for women. Arrangements could be made to connect people of ship needing their services with Association representative on dock.

The Boarding Matrons do not deal with the Steerage unless for example a man, United States Citizen comes to the dock for wife and family in the steerage. They are found and if O.K. by Immigration officer are discharged to the husband through the Boarding Matron.

A man and woman eloped at Stockholm. The woman's husband and her father took a faster steamer and met the eloping party coming ashore. The woman seeing her husband fainted. Boarding Matron perceived an unusual condition, took the matter up with Inspector who learned the facts, delivered the woman to her husband and deported the man.

I have it on good authority that immorality is not confined to the steerage but that many of the stewards and petty officers connected with the 1st, and 2nd. cabin are rotten.

The Process of the Inspection of Alien - Medical

Italy is the only country allowing United States Health Officers to inspect immigrants bound for the United States. These inspectors send home also report of those rejected.

In New York the method of inspections is as follows:-

People of 1st and 2nd cabins not citizens whether coming temporarily on business or pleasure, or to reside are examined and certificates made of defects, if any. This medical certificate is given to Immigration Officer on Board. If the alien satisfies the Inspector that he will not become a public charge, he is permitted to land, otherwise he is brought to Ellis Island for special inquiry.

Aliens coming upon official business from his country is of course, never detained.

Contagious Diseases

In the case [of] aliens suspected of contagious disease, an order is made by the Medical Officer to the Immigration Officer to bring sich [such] alien to Ellis Island for further medical examination.

All these are made on shipboard subjects for the Department of Special Inquiry at Ellis Island. These do not of course go down the line with other steerage passengers for examination.

If upon further examination at Ellis Island they are ordered to the hospital, their valuables are taken and kept by officers in charge of the Medical Division, Ellis Island. When discharged from hospital aliens are again put in charge of Medical Division, valuables are returned and the alien is then given over to an Immigration officer who takes him before the Board of Special Inquiry to determine whether he shall be landed, deferred or excluded. For after physical disability is removed he might have been found to have physical defects other than that for which he was in the hospital, or if clear of physical he might yet have civil defects such as contract, laborer, etc.

If while in hospital it is certified that alien has a contagious disease, his general immigration statement, concerning matters mentioned in the manifest is taken by an Immigration officer in the hospital.

If this statement makes him a subject for special inquiry, the statement and Detention card listing all items are taken to the Board who consider his case while he is still in the hospital.

Temporary contagion like Smallpox, Typhus, etc., are taken off ship at quarantine with as many passengers as the N.Y. Health Officers recommend, but other contagion such as Measles, Diptheria, etc., are kept in the ship's hospital until docked, there reported to U.S. Medical officer who orders them at once to City Hospital. This hospital sends daily report of Patients to Ellis Island, which is given to the rest of the family, if any. This family, in the meantime, is detained there awaiting recovery of patient.

In case of necessity the family is taken to City Hospital to see sick member.

All aliens having permanent contagious diseases are deported. There is no appeal except in cases of disease contracted here and by immigrants going abroad and returning. Such aliens may be landed only by order of Secretary of Commerce & Labor.

If in hospital at Ellis Island an alien suspected of Trachoma is found to have, say, conjunctivitis or Bronchitis instead of tuberculosis etc., he is detained until well, discharged to Medical Division with statement from Hospital Doctors, valuables returned as before described, by this division he is delivered to Immigration Officer who lands him, detains or make special inquiry. Note:- In this report the expression to make S.I. means to bring one into the Department of Special Inquiry and under their absolute control.

Steerage Passengers

When the ship docks, steerage passengers and their baggage are taken on barges to Ellis Island, Immigration officers bring ship's manifest, before described, and medical record.

Passengers are landed at Administration Building, pass up a wide stair case into the center of the great Receiving Room. The first object they see as they come up the steps is a large American flag.

At the top of the stairs their vaccination card is stamped and they pass on for a cursory medical inspection.

Doctor #1 picks out mental suspects making an X with chalk on shoulder and Doctor's initial.

Doctor #2 looks over the general physical condition marking suspected diseases ex. G - Goetre - Scalp disease, H - Hernia, poor physique, L - Lameness, S - Spine disease etc.

Such skill have the doctors in such matters that in case of disease concealed, such as Hernia they are able, I am informed, to pick 98 out of a 100 cases.

Doctor #3 examines eyes marking on shoulder of each Tr. for Trachoma, B. for Blindness, Cat for Cataracts, etc.

Ellis Island is very solicitous concerning Trachoma. Steamship companies are fined $100.00 for every case imported. Last year one company paid $1900.00 in fines.

A Matron stands behind doctors singling our [out] prostitutes and pregnant women whom an inspector makes S.I.

A fourth man turns all those suspects into a cage whence they are taken to another room for careful examination as to diseases suspected. If necessary they are stripped. Should defects prove slight remarks are made on a ticket pinned on vaccination card and they are put in line.

If blemish affects ability to make a living a certificate to that effect is delivered to the Immigration officer who conducts alien into line. Note: the line will be described later.

Immigrants in Medical Room upon examination [who are] found requiring hospital treatment for recovery or suspected of contagious disease are sent to the hospital and go through the process above described in case of 1st. and 2nd. Cabin passengers in hospital.

Mental Cases: If upon examination the alien be found O.K. or very slightly defective Immigration officer turns him into line, otherwise the alien receives a card signed by the examining physician stating cause of holding with remarks, example, A.L.C. stands for

Chronic Alcoholism – Silly expressions – family quarrels – ignorance of days of months, or that 2 & 2 make 4, or apparent nervous disease.

The alien is then taken to another room where a card is filled up [out], giving name, nativity, race, S.S. arrival, group and list number. He is then conducted by Immigration Officer down the line to the registering desk where the Registering Officer gives him a card which conducts him into a special inquiry detention room, whence he comes before a Board of Judges who take his statement, hear witnessess if any defer awaiting further medical examination [sic].

The alien is now delivered to the Deporting Division, and placed in Medical Detention room for observation. He is again examined in the Doctor's office and if O.K. or defects found to be slight a certificate is made to that effect. The medical hold is withdrawn, a statement of the result of examination is made to the S.I. Division which again takes the alien before the Board of Judges. These consider statements of the Doctors and of the aliens and decide to allow alien to land or be bonded or excluded or again deferred for some reason, as for example, awaiting friends.

To bond means that some citizen gives bond in an amount dettermined [sic] at Washington that if admitted the alien will not become a public charge within three years. . . .

Point #1. Where Association could help alien in Detention room.

Note:– Hospital charges and board for people detained are paid by S.S. company at rate of 24¢ per day for food, $1.25 to $1.75 for hospital; for care of insane patients in asylums at this time until ship sails $5.00 per day.

The Line

If in the beginning the alien passes the Doctors he is taken by an employs [sic] called a Grouper and placed in line of 30's according to the number on his ship's card pinned on his coat. Ex. there are 30 – 1's and 30 – 2's, etc.

At the end of each line is a desk upon which the ship's manifest is spread out. There is a registering officer and interpreter.

Registering consists in checking off questions stated in manifest before alluded to, and accounts to a further shifting of the aliens. If any are found undesirable or apparently not within the law they are sent to the S.I. Detention Room to go to before the Board. These immigrants, be remembered, were passed by doctors. . . .

Point #2. Where Association man might help the alien.

It is the policy of Ellis Island to keep families intact so far as possible. Should one member be detained for observation or hospital treatment the rest of the family are usually detained or paroled to some society. . . .

Point #3. In case of men, Associations could arrange to undertake this. Association can help in the Detention Room.

If alien is O'ked, at Register's desk, has enough money and order for transportation to destination, he is passed on by a series of employes [*sic*] out into corridors down stairs to Railroad Room where all Railroad and steamship lines are represented.

Here he changes his money to U.S. currency, gets Railroad ticket, is placed in proper pen and later the whole company is taken by Immigration officer on barges to proper Railroad station or dock.

This is the only place where Y.M.C.A. is at present working.

Aliens OK.ed by Registering officer going to New York, who are to be met by relatives or friends or are waiting for money are temporarily detained pending the coming of friends, telegraphing for money, etc. These receive a special card and are placed in the New York Detention room.

Here the Association man could be useful.

Aliens found by Registering inspector to have an unfavorable medical report or otherwise suspected of being unfit for landing are sent to Special Inquiry Department. Should there be witnesses, their testimony is taken before seeing the alien friend.

Y.M.C.A. could help at this point by representing aliens and preventing misconception.

Should there not be sufficient evidence to admit or exclude or a probability of further proof, the alien is deferred, taken out to Deporting Division, which has charge of all cases deferred or excluded.

Association man could help the alien at this point by assisting him to communicate with his friends and explaining methods at Ellis Island and helping aliens to take advantage of rights allowed by law.

After five days deferred cases must be taken up, sometimes final action is then taken or the case then again be deferred.

Should testimony arrive before the five day limit[,] case is taken up at once.

Association men could help here [with their] sympathetic knowledge of men and methods.

When Board of Judges decides that a case under the law should be excluded, the alien is delivered to Deporting Division.

The Deporting Division has charge of alines [aliens] detained, held for medical examination or to be excluded. It is their duty to convey members of a detained family to [the] hospital either at Ellis Island or [to the] City Hospital to see sick members and to deport upon order of Commiss[i]oner or Secretary of Commerce & Labor.

In case the Board decides for exclusion, an appeal can be taken through the Commissioner to the Secretary of Commerce & Labor showing cause why alien will not become a public charge, asking to bond or [to] re-open case.

An Association man would naturally attend to this matter in cases of young men.

It sometimes happens that the Board decides for exclusion but recommends bonding. This must of course be done through Washington. All this and kindred matters could be attended to by Association representatives as they are being done to a degree by representatives of other agencies.

The point is this--a man detained or in danger of exclusion is inclined to be more grateful to the YMCA than when free to depart merely receives a card of introduction in the Railroad rooms.

Baggage

All baggage comes off the ship with the immigrant and is taken to Ellis Island. Those going to Railroad deliver the brass check received from the Baggage Master on ship, to baggage master in Railroad room, giving address, etc., as in the case of ordinary travel.

Those going elsewhere, having finished in the Railroad room, on the way to Railroad pen, pass through Baggage room, giving up brass check receive paper check and pick out baggage which is then forwarded.

Association could help here perhaps, but not a great deal.

APPENDIX B-5

EYE WITNESS ACCOUNT OF CONDITIONS OF STEERAGE

PASSENGERS ABOARD IMMIGRANT TRANSPORT

Report from a Mr. James, YMCA Worker, to E. S. Towson

Mr. James is a registered seaman who made a trip of investigation in the steerage of the Hamburg-American Line.

I spent considerable time with Mr. James. He was good enough to allow me to make note of his experiences which I have put together, as follows:-

Mr. James was sent officially by the Brooklyn Association, by the Immigration class of about one hundred, Mr. Scott, Physical Director, Brooklyn Association, being the Leader.

He was given $115.00 for the trip;
His passage cost	$ 75.00
Picture expenses	15.00
Baggage, etc.	5.00
In Germany	8.00
	$103.00

He wrote Mr. Scott from Germany and immediately upon returning also called several times at the Brooklyn, Y.M.C.A. and found him away.

Mr. James took steerage passage out on the "S.S" "Graf Walderse [sic] under [the] name of Gaurl Bauman. For the first two days he merely observed the general condition of the ship.

There were ninety steerage passengers, beside a number working their way as coal trimmers etc.

After two days came in touch with passengers; found some of those returning had been in this country from two to four years, five or six were being deported; two Jews were returning with consumption, being unable to pay high fees of doctors here: most of those returning were shabbily dressed.

Almost every man complained about hard work in America and exorbitant Doctors bills. Found them quite ignorant of America[n] ideals and constitution. Only one could speak any English having gone to school eight months. Two little boys had a touch of Americanism, these children of six and seven were superior to the rest.

One Immigrant going home said, "This president good, plenty work - bye and bye new president - no work for me."

One coming this way had letter from Brother in Pittsburg saying "meat every day as much as you like, plenty beer, plenty whiskey."

One man was made infidel by priests. A girl going home to care for parents told rough tales of Polish priest in America.

An Austrian here five years, a citizen, spoke broken English, enthusiastic about America.

Deported Roum[a]nian lay in bunk crying day after day "Oh God, Oh God what shall I do, all my money gone." Agents promise money back if deported. A petty officer told Mr. James this promise is not kept.

A Hungarian lady, thirteen years in American [sic] returning, complained of Roman Catholic Church here, not like Church at home in spirit and morality.

Several Jews said they lost faith of fathers in America because compelled to work on Sabbath.

Mr. James spread Christian Jewish tracts when advisable and testified concerning the Christian faith whenever possible, and held service in Second cabin.

The small number of passengers afforded opportunity for games, etc.

A horse was quartered twelve feet from tables in the dining room, there was no box stall, upon complaint of passengers it was shut off by canvass.

Going out the food was good, but service bad. A sailor steward dragged in baskets of rolls, shoves them along the tables shouting essen[tially] - eat is that enough - ten gallon pot of butter and sails this across the table.

Half the toilet rooms were roped off to save cleaning, five left open.

Women's wash-room freely entered by between deck stewards. One woman said she repeatedly saw half-naked stewards washing themselves in there because it was cleaner than the mens' wash-rooms.

One woman was waked up by steward on duty whom she put to flight with her shoes.

Mr. James landed in Hamburg, visited the Y.M.C.A., made addresses spent a week at home.

In Rotterdam investigated Holland-American-Line - found it much improved since he sailed an emigrant ten years ago. Larger ships, better accommodation for steerage - on some ships state room for steerage, dining rooms on all and good service and district [sic] discipline.

Mr. James believes much of what he complains of is due to lax discipline.

He learned that employe[e]s of the Russian-American fleet ship people detained and refused by the Holland-American Line at Rotterdam and smuggle them off at New York.

From Rotterdam he proceeded to Hamburg to start for America.

The Hamburg American Line have barracks there for people arriving before the ship sails.

The City has a large hotel for this pripose [sic] at Rotterdam, the medical inspection is severe, at Hamburg it is lax. They try to treat eyes to last until past Ellis Island.

He went into the Waiting Room, passed medical inspection, was taken with other emigrants in small steamer to the Batavia coming aboard of which rude treatment began, cursing and driving.

The immigrants were divided into groups supposedly according to Nationality, James was sent among the Poles, asked steward to show where Germans were, "Find them yourself" he replied.

A married man was separated from wife and daughter, tried to get with them, but was forbidden. Mr. James did not know whether he finally succeeded; families are not supposed to be separated.

Mr. James remarked that in embarking he had sold his liberty for seventeen long days and added that the steerage as he saw it is not a good introduction to the land of liberty.

While the immigrants could not be treated as refined educated people, or those traveling first class, they should be treated more like human beings than was the case on this trip.

Second Cabin fare is 200 Marks, Steerage 150 Marks, the difference is usually spent at the bar because the food and water are bad.

Compartments 50 x 65 and 80 x 65 contain from 175 to 290 beds, these are iron frame, double tired [tiered] and in blocks of 32.

The floor of the deck is of iron and so necessarily damp. Electric lights were too dim for reading.

The one blanket proved too little on a cold night. On a certain night the 1st and 2nd Cabins with plenty of bed clothing had steam heat, the steerage had none; they asked for heat, but it was not given.

There were no clthes [sic] hooks, or lockers, no place for baggage except the floor which was always unclean with refuse or vomit; so the bed becomes cupboard for dishes and baggage.

The tables set in the alleys consisted of boards on trestles. There were no dining rooms, no cuspidors, no slop buckets.

Repeated complaint was made to the captain about the food.

One day all the Jews piled their utensils on the deck and went to complain to the Captain.

Coffee was poor, half of the potatoes had to be thrown away.

The kettle for drinking water was not refilled unless the Steward felt like it and the piteous cry for water was constantly heard.

The fresh water faucett was turned off much of the time.

Meals were not served. Every sixteenth man had a card and went for the food for his squad. If he did not bring the right kind or amount and returned he was refused as he was marked served.

There was no warm fresh water for washing, but cold seawater, in which it is impossible to clean anything especially greasy dishes. Dishes were washed in washbowl of the toilet room; some washed them at deck wash-pipe, but Boatswain rudely objected to this.

The absolute hooror [sic] of all this appears when it is said that the wash rooms and toilet rooms were too few and too small. All day long there was a line of people waiting to get into the toilet rooms, and that a woman was seen coming from a wash room with excrement on her feet.

The only fresh water available for washing had to be stolen from the galley.

There were sixteen stewards, eight for day and eight for night and three stewardesses for 15000 passengers. Once they were all drunk. As a result from fight two were imprisoned. Two sailors fought with knives trying to sleep between women passengers.

Two cases of Kramel [sic] whiskey were found under a bed in the steerage being sold to passengers at exorbitant prices. Many boys were drunk.

In general the males were cuffed and vulgar remarks and vulgar actions addressed to females.

No single female was free from the vulgarity of the crew; it must be admitted that some liked it.

Attractive females would receive a meal from the cook or a bottle of wine from a fireman.

"Do not spit on the floor to avoid consumption" was conspicuously posted about the steerage, but no receptacles, whether spitoons or slop buckets were provided.

Women are followed all day by immoral crew, whether or not they yield is up to them. But a ship that receives people for transport should certainly protect them from their own crew.

The steerage was washed only once during the trip of seventeen days.

The ship's kindness reached the extent of giving candy and tobacco as a means of restraint. They held back their tickets without, which, of course, the emigrants could not land.

Mr. James complained to captain about second Cabin's Obscenity to two girls whom he tried to protect. Captain ordered James to be taken to the 1st officer, but was taken to Chief Steward instead. Nothing resulted so far as he could learn.

The two women were followed all day by cooks, quarter-masters, etc., even by Doctor. Later he saw these two in Quarter-master's room at 11:30 P.M. among empty beer bottles, the Quarter-master asleep on the lounge. These were German girls, one going to Iron Mountains, Tenn., and the other to Milwaukee. They seemed all right at first but probably succumed to constant and insistent temptation in the unnatural life of being on ship board. . . .

Two Russian ladies paid 80 Marks to get into Second Cabin.

James fed an officer to allow him to eat and sleep in his room.

Vaccination was as follows:- Driven between decks, all hatches but one were closed. The air became so unbearable that some broke open a hatch and escaped. Nevertheless these got their vaccination card stamped. 1800 were vaccinated in four hours, same instrument was used on eight with[out] cleansing.

A man whose whole side was swollen from vaccination had arm treated not with distilled water but with water from tank.

Compared to the steerage as James saw it, Ellis Island is heaven itself.

Mr. James makes the following suggestions:-

1. American law should not permit so many passengers in steerage that such conditions should be possible.
2. Decks should be of wood to avoid cold and dampness.
3. While there is one waiter to six in first Cabin; one to twelve in second Cabin; there is one to 200 in the Steerage.
[4]. Ship ought to wash dishes and serve meals, bringing the food to passengers.
5. There should be bath rooms at least for mothers with babies.
6. Dining rooms should be provided.
7. Men specially detailed to keep toilet and washrooms clean.
8. Divide steerage wholly or in part into staterooms.
9. Plenty of fresh water. This can be gotten for cattle why not for people.
10. No liquor to crew or passengers, beer perhaps to those regarding it as a necessity.
11. Nothing should be sold by the employe[e]s except in the canteens.
12. No tips.
13. Severe discipline for the protection of women.
14. A book wherein the complaints of the passengers may be registered.
15. An intermediate class between 2nd Cabin and steerage as on the "America," "Augusta," and "Victoria."

No knives, no forks, no table cloths, no dining room, no spitoons, no refuse buckets, add to this whoremonger crew certainly is not a square deal for the poor female emigrant.

Steerage people strange to say were very religious for the reason that large percentage were Jews and Roman Catholics.

The Jews put certain prayer paraphernalia upon their arms and upon their foreheads, standing in a row they prayed for an hour each morning.

The Catholics assembled in groups kissing pictures of the Virgin or crucifixes or amulets or hold a song service, but their religion did not prevent immoral conversation, drunkness and grossly obscene actions quite unfit to describe.

An Association worker or Chaplin would need to be a phenominal linguist. A man of required talents could not stand the constant strain the steerage would impose upon his sympathies. His work might be hampered by Roman Catholics and Jews; certainly in the matter of protecting females he would antagonize the crew to the extent of endangering his life. Still it would be a noble work if a man qualified to speak the languages and deal with the people could be found. The prospect of danger would not prove an obstacle to the average American.

Some of the recommendations of Mr. James are in force on some liners, notably relating to State Room on one and to liquor [on] another.

BIBLIOGRAPHY

UNPUBLISHED MATERIALS

Industrial Immigrant Work Materials, 1900-1930. Y.M.C.A. Historical Library, New York City.

Peter Roberts Materials. Y.M.C.A. Historical Library, New York City.

Reports of the Industrial Committee of the Young Men's Christian Association, 1900-1920. Y.M.C.A. Historical Library, New York City.

GOVERNMENT DOCUMENTS

Commonwealth of Massachusetts Public Documents. *Annual Reports of Various Public Officers and Institutions - Education, 1907-1917*. Boston: Wright and Potter Printing Company, State Printers.

New York State. *Department of Education Annual Reports*. New York Assembly Documents 1907-1917.

Pennsylvania, State of. *Reports of the Superintendent of Public Instruction*, 1907-1917.

U.S. Bureau of Education. *Education of the Immigrant*. Bulletin No. 51. Washington, 1913.

U.S. Bureau of Education. *The Fitchburg Plan of Industrial Education*. Bulletin No. 50. Washington, 1913.

U.S. Bureau of Education. *Types of Apprentice Systems*. Bulletin No. 6. Washington, 1908.

U.S. Commissioner of Labor. *Industrial Education*. Twenty-fifth Annual Report, 1910. Washington, 1911.

U.S. House of Representatives. *Report of the Commission on National Aid to Vocational Education*. House Document 1004, 63rd Congress, 2nd Session, 1913-1914. Washington, 1914.

U.S. Immigration Commission. *Statements by Societies Interested in Immigration*. Sen. Doc. 23, 61st Congress, 2nd Session, 1910-1911.

ARTICLES

Abbott, Ernest H. "Christian Pagans." *Outlook*, LXXXI (December 16, 1905), 917-21.

_____. "The Exodus from Philistia." *Outlook*, LXXXI (December 30, 1905), 1073-77.

Addams, Jane. "The Subtle Problems of Charity." *Atlantic Monthly*, LXXXIII (February, 1899), 163-78.

"An Adventure in Public Opinion." *Outlook*, CII (September 7, 1912), 42.

Baruch, Bertha. "Report before the Patriots League." *The Survey*, XXVIII (September 14, 1912), 748.

Boas, Franz. "Changes in Bodily Form of the Descendants of Immigrants." In U.S. Immigration Commission. *Reports*, XXXVIII. Serial 5063. Washington, 1911.

Bourne, Randolf. "Trans National America." *Atlantic Monthly*, CXVIII (July, 1916), 86-97.

Bradley, A. A. "To What Extent Does Unrestricted Immigration Counteract the Influence of Our Educational and Charitable Work." *Charities*, VIII (April 5, 1902), 325-30.

Bremer, Edith Terry. "Development of Private Social Work with the Foreign Born." *Annals of the American Academy of Political and Social Science*, CCLXII (March, 1949), 139-47.

_____. "Foreign Community and Immigration Work of the National Young Women's Christian Association." *The Immigrants in America Review*, I (January, 1916), 73-82.

"Care of Dependent Children." *Charities*, VII (November 2, 1901), 368-74.

Cates, E. E. "The Teaching of History in the Secondary Schools." *Education*, XXXIV (April, 1914), 491-500.

Cohen, Sol. "The Industrial Education Movement." *American Quarterly* XX (Spring, 1968), 95-110.

Conway, Jill. "Jane Addams: An American Heroine." *The Woman in America*. Robert J. Lifton, ed. Boston: Little, Brown & Co., 1965.

Crum, Frederick C. "The Decadence of the Native American Stock: A Statistical Study of Geneological Records." *Publications of the American Statistical Association*, XIV (September, 1914), 218-19.

Ellenwood, Charles A. "Our Compulsory Education Laws and Retardation." *Education*, XXXIV (May, 1914), 572-76.

Engineering News, LXVII. Editorial (January 4, 1912), 35.

Frank, Waldo. "The Beverly Factory Industrial School Plan." *Education*, XXXV (March, 1915), 434-43.

Gregg, H. F. M. "Social Hygiene." *Education*, XXXIII (October, 1912), 100-104.

"A Great Instrument." *Outlook*, LXXII (September 6, 1902), 14-15.

Hackett, Francis. "As an Alien Feels." *New Republic*, III (July 24, 1915), 303-306.

Halsey, Edward A. "Our Brothers the Immigrants." *The World Today*, XIX (December, 1910), 1375-81.

Heald, Morrell. "Business Attitudes Toward European Immigration 1880-1900." *Journal of Economic History*, XIII (Summer, 1953), 290-304.

Herzfeld, Elsa G. "Superstitions and Customs of the Tenement House Mother." *Charities*, XIV (August 5, 1905), 983-86.

Higham, John. "Origins of Immigration Restriction 1882-1897: A Social Analysis." *Mississippi Valley Historical Review*, XXXIX (June, 1952), 77-88.

Hodge, George. "On Pauperism." *Charities*, II (December 3, 1898), 7.

Holmes, S. J., and Dodd, C. M. "The Approaching Extinction of the Mayflower Decendents." *Journal of Heredity*, IX (November, 1918), 296-300.

Howe, Oliver H. "Cultural Education." *Education*, XXXIV (January, 1914), 320-27.

Howe, Samuel B. "History in the Elementary Schools." *Education*, XXXIII (June, 1914), 638-45.

Hunsaker, A. F. "Civics in the Secondary Schools." *Education*, XXXIII (December, 1912), 228-37.

"Industrial Service, New York City." *The Intercollegian*, XXXII (June, 1910), 254-56.

Johnston, Charles H. "The Nation as a Participant in Popular Education." *Education Administration and Supervision*, I (February, 1915), 154-56.

Lodge, Henry Cabot. "Census and Immigration." *Century Magazine*, XLVI (September, 1893), 737-39.

_____. "Lynch Law and Unrestricted Immigration." *North American Review*, CLII (May, 1891), 602-12.

_____. "The Restriction of Immigration." *North American Review*, CLII (January, 1891), 27-36.

Lynd, Staughton. "Jane Addams and the Radical Impulse." *Commentary*, XXXII (July, 1961), 54-59.

Mahy, M. Catherine. "The Differentiation of Teaching English Classes in the High School." *Education*, XXXVI (May, 1916), 574-80.

Mann, Arthur. "Gompers and the Irony of Racism." *Antioch Review*, XIII (Summer, 1953), 203-14.

McCook, John J. "The Work of the Y.M.C.A. Among Railroad Men." *The Jubilee of Work for Young Men in North America*. New York: Jubilee Convention of North American Young Men's Christian Associations, 1908.

Michener, C. C. "Industrial Y.M.C.A.'s Work." *Textile Manufacturer's Journal* (December 29, 1906), 97.

Miller, Kelly. "Moral Pedagogy." *Education*, XXXIV (November, 1913), 133-44.

Molter, Harold. "Practical Suggestions for the Teaching of Sex Hygiene." *Education*, XXXIV (October, 1913), 95-98.

"Night Schools for Americanizing Immigrants." *The Immigrants in America Review*, II (April, 1916), 35-37.

Paine, Robert T. "The Importance of Stopping Outdoor Relief to Chronic or Hereditary Paupers." *Charities*, X (February 7, 1903), 134-37.

Persons, W. Frank. "Reading for the Poor." *Charities*, VIII (May 3, 1902), 416-22.

Peterson, Jon A. "From Social Work to Social Agency: Settlement Work In Columbus, Ohio 1898-1958." *Social Science Review*, XXXIX (June, 1965), 191-208.

Roberts, Norman. "Part Time Training." *Engineering News*, LXVII (February 8, 1912), 260.

Roberts, Peter. "The Ethnic Factors in Immigrants to North America." In Illinois Miners and Mechanics Institute, *Bulletin No. 3*. Urbana: University of Illinois Press, 1914, 24-36.

_____. "The Roberts Method of Teaching English to Foreigners." In Illinois Miners and Mechanics Institute, *Bulletin No. 3*. Urbana: University of Illinois Press, 1914, 37-40.

_____. "The Y.M.C.A. Among the Immigrants." *Survey*, XXIX (February 15, 1913), 697-700.

_____. "The Y.M.C.A. Teaching Foreign Speaking Men." *The Immigrants in America Review*, I (June, 1915), 18-23.

Ross, Edward A. "The Causes of Racial Superiority." *Annals of the American Academy of Political and Social Science*, XVIII (July, 1901), 67-89.

Rousmaniere, John P. "Cultural Hybrid in the Slums: The College Woman and the Settlement House." *American Quarterly*, XXII (Spring, 1970), 45-66.

Sleet, J. C. "A Successful Experiment." *Charities*, VI (January 5, 1901), 2-5.

Smith, Timothy L. "Immigrant Social Aspirations and American Education." *American Quarterly* XXI (Fall, 1969), 523-43.

Solomon, Barbara. "The Intellectual Background of the Immigration Restriction Movement in the Northeast." *Northeast Quarterly*, XXV (March, 1952), 47-59.

The Student Volunteer. Y.M.C.A. Publication, 1900-1917.

Thomas, W. I. "Five Polish Peasant Letters." *The Immigrants in America Review*, II (April, 1916), 58-63.

Todd, Edwin S. "An Economic Basis for Civics Teaching." *Education*, XXXII (March, 1912), 436-44.

Tucker, William J. "Twenty-five Years in Residence." *Atlantic Monthly*, CXIX (May, 1917), 640-49.

Vaughn, S. J. "The Moral Significance of the Vocational Motive." *Education*, XXXIII (June, 1913), 591-603.

Walker, Francis A. "Immigration and Degradation." *Forum*, XI (August, 1891), 634-44.

Wharton, George W. "Business Men at School." *Outlook*, LXXXVII (October 12, 1907), 303-306.

Whiton, James M. "The Jubilee Convention of Young Men's Christian Associations." *Outlook*, LXVIII (July 6, 1901), 586-92.

Wiebe, Robert H. "The Social Functions of Public Education." *American Quarterly*, XXI (Summer, 1969), 147-64.

"Work Among Italian Immigrants." *Charities*, IX (February 7, 1903), 122-24.

"Young Men's Christian Association Annual Dinner." *Outlook*, LXXXIV (November 17, 1917), 648.

BOOKS AND PUBLISHED PROCEEDINGS

Adair, Ward. *Memories of George Warburton*. New York: J. J. Little and Ives and Company, n.d.

Addams, Jane. *Democracy and Social Ethics*. New York: Macmillan, 1902.

_____. *My Friend Julia Lathrop*. New York: Macmillan, 1935.

_____. *The Second Twenty Years at Hull House*. New York: Macmillan, 1930.

_____. *Social Control*, No. 4. New York: Publication of the National Association for the Advancement of Colored People, n.d.

_____. *Twenty Years at Hull House*. New York: Macmillan, 1911.

Arendt, Hannah. *The Origins of Totalitarianism*. New York: Harcourt, Brace and World, 1966.

Arthur, George R. *Life on the Negro Frontier*. New York: Association Press, 1934.

Ayres, Leonard P. *Laggards in Our Schools*. New York: Charities Publishing Company, 1909.

Begbie, Harold. *The Ordinary Man and the Extraordinary Thing*. New York: G. H. Doran, 1912.

Boas, Franz. *The Mind of Primitive Man*. New York: Macmillan, 1911.

Brace, Charles Loring. *The Dangerous Classes of New York and Twenty Years Among Them*. New York: Wyncoop and Hallenbeck, 1872.

Bremner, Robert H. *From the Depths*. New York: University Press, 1956.

Carey, Clifford M., ed. *Between Two Centuries, Report of the Centennial International Young Men's Christian Association Convention*. New York: Association Press, 1951.

Cole, William I. *Motives and Results of the Settlement Movement*. Cambridge, Massachusetts: Harvard University Department of Social Ethics, 1908.

Commons, John R. *Race and Immigration in America*. New York: Macmillan, 1920.

Daniels, Roger. *The Politics of Prejudice*. Los Angeles: University of California Press, 1962.

Davis, Allan F. *Spearheads for Reform*. New York: Oxford, 1967.

Dedmon, Emmett. *Great Enterprises*. New York: Rand McNally, 1957.

Doggett, L. L. *The Life of Robert R. McBurney*. Cleveland, Ohio: F. M. Barton Company, 1902.

Donoghue, Terry. *An Event on Mercer Street*. Place not given, privately printed, n.d.

Dooley, William H. *The Education of the Ne'er-Do-Well*. Boston: Houghton Mifflin, 1916.

Drury, Clifford M. *San Francisco Y.M.C.A., One Hundred Years by the Golden Gate, 1853-1953*. Glendale, Calif.: A. H. Clark and Company, 1963.

East, Edward M. *Heredity and Human Affairs*. New York: C. Scribners Sons, 1927.

Eddy, George S. *A Century with Youth*. New York: Association Press, 1944.

Ellenwood, James L. *Look at the "Y"*. New York: Association Press, 1940.

Ely, Richard T. *The Labor Movement in America*. New York: Thomas Y. Crowell and Company, 1886.

Farrell, John C. *Beloved Lady*. Baltimore: Johns Hopkins Press, 1967.

Fink, Arthur E. *Causes of Crime: Biological Theories in the United States 1800-1915*. Philadelphia: University of Pennsylvania Press, 1938.

Fisher, Galen. *Public Affairs and the Y.M.C.A.* New York: Association Press, 1948.

Fiske, John. *The Beginnings of New England: or The Puritan Theocracy in Its Relation to Civil and Religious Liberty*. Boston and New York: Houghton Mifflin, 1899.

_____. *The Critical Period in American History*. Boston and New York: Houghton Mifflin, 1916.

_____. *Old Virginia and Her Neighbors*. 2 vols. Boston and New York: Houghton Mifflin, 1902.

Foerster, Robert F. *Italian Immigration of Our Times*. Cambridge, Massachusetts: Harvard University Press, 1924.

Ford, James. *Slums and Housing*. 2 vols. Cambridge, Massachusetts: Harvard University Press, 1936.

Gossett, Thomas F. *Race: The History of an Idea in America*. Dallas, Texas: Southern Methodist University Press, 1963.

Goldman, Eric F. *Rendevous with Destiny*. New York: Alfred A. Knopf, 1965.

Grant, Madison. *The Passing of the Great Race*. New York: C. Scribners Sons, 1916.

Greenslet, Ferris. *The Life of Thomas Bailey Aldrich*. Boston and New York: Houghton Mifflin, 1908.

Gross, Howard B. *Aliens or Americans*. New York: Young People's Missionary Movement of the United States and Canada, 1906.

Haldane, John B. S. *Heredity and Politics*. New York: W. W. Norton, 1938.

Hall, Prescott F. *Immigration and its Effects Upon the United States*. New York: H. Holt and Company, 1906.

Haller, Mark. *Eugenics: Hereditarian Attitudes in American Thought*. New Brunswick, N.J.: Rutgers University, 1963.

Handlin, Oscar. *Immigration as a Factor in American History*. Englewood Cliffs, N.J.: Prentice Hall, 1959.

_____. *Race and Nationality in American Life*. Boston: Little, Brown and Company, 1948.

Hapgood, Hutchins. *The Anarchist Woman*. New York: Duffield and Company, 1909.

_____. *Four Poets of the Ghetto*. Berkeley Heights, N.J.: Oriole Press, 1963.

_____. *The Spirit of the Ghetto*. Cambridge: Massachusetts: Harvard University Press, 1967.

_____. *The Spirit of Labor*. New York: Duffield and Company, 1907.

_____. *Types from City Streets*. New York: Funk and Wagnalls, 1910.

Hartmann, Edward George. *The Movement to Americanize the Immigrant*. New York: Columbia University Press, 1948.

Hays, Samuel P. *The Response to Industrialism*. Chicago: University of Chicago Press, 1959.

Higham, John. *Strangers in the Land*. New Brunswick, N.J.: Rutgers, 1955.

Hofstadter, Richard. *The Age of Reform*. New York: Alfred A. Knopf, 1955.

_____. *Social Darwinism in American Thought*. New York: Braziller, 1959.

Holden, Arthur C. *The Settlement Idea*. New York: Macmillan, 1922.

Hopkins, Charles Howard. *History of the Y.M.C.A. In North America*. New York: Association Press, 1951.

Howe, Frederick C. *The City: Hope of Democracy*. New York: Scribners, 1905.

Hughes, Rupert. *The Real New York*. New York: Smart Set Publishing Company, 1904.

Hull House Residents. *Hull House Maps and Papers*. New York: Thomas Y. Crowell, 1895.

Hunter, Robert. *Poverty*. New York: Macmillan, 1909.

Illinois Miners and Mechanics Institute. *Bulletin No. 3*. Urbana: University of Illinois Press, 1914.

International Survey of Young Men's and Young Women's Christian Associations. New York: International Survey Committee, 1932.

Jefferson, Charles E. *Essentials*. New York: Association Press, 1908.

Jones, M. Allen. *American Immigration*. Chicago: University of Chicago Press, 1960.

Jordan, David Starr. *The Human Harvest: A Study of the Decay of Races Through the Survival of the Unfit*. Boston: American Unitarian Association, 1907.

_____. *Imperial Democracy*. New York: D. Appleton, 1899.

Jubilee of Work for Young Men in North America. New York: International Committee of Young Men's Christian Associations, 1901.

Kallen, Horace M. *Culture and Democracy in the United States*. New York: Boni and Liverwright, 1924.

Kelley, Edmund. *The Elimination of the Tramp*. New York: Putnam's Sons, 1908.

Korman, Gerd. *Industrialization, Immigrants, and Americanizers*. Madison, Wisconsin: The State Historical Society of Wisconsin, 1967.

Lasch, Christopher. *The New Radicalism in America 1889-1963*. New York: Vintage Press, 1967.

Levine, Daniel. *Varieties of Reform Thought*. Stephens Point, Wisconsin: Worzalla Publishing Company, 1964.

Link, Arthur S. *Woodrow Wilson and the Progressive Era*. New York: Harper, 1954.

Linn, James W. *Jane Addams*. New York: Greenwood Press, 1963.

Lodge, Henry Cabot. *Early Memories*. New York: Macmillan, 1913.

_____. *A Short History of the English Colonies in America*. New York: Macmillan, 1881.

Lord, Eliot, et al. *The Italian in America*. New York: B. F. Buck and Company, 1905.

Lubove, Roy. *The Professional Altruist*. Cambridge, Massachusetts: Harvard University Press, 1965.

_____. *The Progressive and the Slums*. New York: Harper Row, 1964.

May, Henry F. *The End of American Innocence*. New York: Alfred A. Knopf, 1959.

_____. *Protestant Churches and Industrial America*. New York: Harper, 1949.

McKelvey, Blake. *The Urbanization of America*. New Brunswick, N.J.: Rutgers University Press, 1963.

Morse, Richard C. *History of North American Y.M.C.A.'s*. New York: Association Press, 1913.

_____. *My Life With Young Men*. New York: Association Press, 1918.

Mott, John R. *The Students of North America United*. New York: International Committee of Young Men's Christian Associations, 1903.

National Conference of Charities and Corrections. *Proceedings 1900-1918*.

National Society for the Promotion of Industrial Education. *Proceedings, 1907-1918*. New York: various printers.

New York East Side House. *Reports 1892-1909*. New York: B. H. Tyrell Printer, n.d.

New York State Conference of Charities and Corrections. *Proceedings 1900-1917*. Albany: J. B. Lyon Company.

North America Civic League for Immigrants. *Annual Report, 1913-1914*. Boston: N.A.C.L., 1914.

_____. *Messages for New Comers to the United States.* Boston: N.A.C.L., n.d.

Ober, Frank W. *James Stokes, Pioneer.* New York: Association Press, 1921.

Park, Robert E. *Race and Culture.* Glencoe, Illinois: Free Press, 1950.

_____, and Miller, Herbert A. *Old World Traits Transplanted.* New York: Harper and Brothers, 1921.

Parmalee, Maurice. *Poverty and Social Progress.* New York: Macmillan, 1916.

Pence, Owen. *The Y.M.C.A. and Social Need: A Study of Institutional Adaptation.* New York: Association Press, 1946.

Popenoe, Paul and Gosney, E. S. *Twenty-eight Years of Sterilization In California.* Pasadena: Human Betterment Foundation, 1938.

Public Utility Economics. New York: West Side Young Men's Christian Association, 1914.

Riis, Jacob. *Children of the Poor.* New York: C. Scribners Sons, 1893.

_____. *Children of the Tenements.* New York: Macmillan, 1903.

_____. *How The Other Half Lives.* New York: Scribner, 1890.

Ripley, William Z. *The Races of Europe.* New York: D. Appleton and Company, 1899.

Roberts, Peter. *Civics for Coming Americans.* New York: Association Press, 1912.

_____. *Civics for Coming Americans.* New York: Association Press, 1917.

_____. *English for Coming Americans, Advanced Course, First Reader.* New York: Association Press, 1918.

_____. *English for Coming Americans, Second Reader.* New York: Association Press, 1912.

_____. *English for Coming Americans, Teacher's Aids.* New York: Association Press, 1912.

_____. *English for Coming Canadians, Teacher's Manual.* New York: Association Press, 1912.

_____. *English Reader for Use in Cantonment Areas.* New York: Association Press, 1917.

_____. *English Reading Lessons.* New York: Young Men's Christian Association Industrial Department, 1917.

Ross, Edward A. *The Old World and the New.* New York: Century, 1914.

_____. *Changing America.* New York: Century, 1912.

Saveth, Edward N. *American Historians and European Immigrants 1875-1925*. New York: Russell and Russell, 1965.

Simkhovitch, Mary K. *Neighborhood*. New York: W. W. Norton Publishing Company, 1938.

Smith, Charles Sprague. *Working with the People*. New York: A. Wessels Company, 1908.

Smith, Mayo. *Emigration and Immigration*. New York: Macmillan, 1890.

Solomon, Barbara. *Ancestors and Immigrants*. Cambridge, Massachusetts: Harvard University Press, 1956.

Sorenson, Roy, and Dimock, Hedley S. *Designing Education Values*. New York: Association Press, 1955.

Steffens, Lincoln. *The Autobiography of Lincoln Steffens*. New York: Harcourt Brace and Company, 1931.

Super, Paul. *Training A Staff*. New York: Association Press, 1920.

Taylor, Graham W. *Pioneering on New Social Frontiers*. Chicago: University of Chicago Press, 1930.

Tims, Margaret. *Jane Addams of Hull House*. London: Allen and Unwin, 1961.

Turner, Fredrick Jackson. *The Frontier in American History*. New York: Holt, Rinehart and Winston, 1962.

Wald, Lillian. *The House on Henry Street*. New York: Henry Holt and Company, 1915.

_____. *Windows on Henry Street*. Boston: Little, Brown and Company, 1941.

Warner, Amos G. *American Charities*. New York: Thomas Y. Crowell, 1908.

_____, Queen, Stuart A., and Harper, Ernest B. *American Charities and Social Work*. New York: Thomas Y. Crowell, 1919.

Watson, Frank D. *The Charity Organization Movement in the United States*. New York: Macmillan, 1922.

White, Morton. *Social Thought in America*. New York: Viking Press, 1949.

Whiteside, William B. *The Boston Y.M.C.A. and the Community Need - A Century's Evolution 1851-1951*. New York: Association Press, 1951.

Wiebe, Robert H. *The Search for Order 1877-1920*. New York: Hill and Wang, 1967.

Wiener, Norbert. *Ex-Prodigy: My Childhood and Youth*. New York: Simon and Shuster, 1953.

Wilson, Woodrow. *A History of the American People, IV*. New York: Harper Brothers, 1902.

Wittke, Carl. *We Who Built America*. New York: Prentice Hall, 1939.

Woodroofe, Kathleen. *From Charity to Social Work*. Toronto: University of Toronto Press, 1966.

Woods, Elenore. *Robert Woods, Champion of Democracy*. Boston: Little, Brown, 1929.

Woods, Frances J. *Cultural Values in American Ethnic Groups*. New York: Harper, 1956.

Woods, Robert A., ed. *Americans in Process*. New York: Houghton Mifflin, 1903.

_____, and Kennedy, Albert J. *The Settlement Horizon - A National Estimate*. New York: Russell Sage Foundation, 1922.